International Directory
of Renaissance and Reformation
Associations and Institutes

International Directory
of Renaissance and Reformation
Associations and Institutes

Compiled by

Konrad Eisenbichler
Lesley B. Cormack
Jacqueline Murray

Toronto
Centre for Reformation and Renaissance Studies
1990

Canadian Cataloguing-in-Publication Data

Eisenbichler, Konrad.
   International directory of Renaissance and Reformation associations
and institutes

Includes some text in French.
ISBN 0–7727–2013–4

1. Research institutes — Directories. 2. Renaissance —
Research — Directories. 3. Reformation — Research —
Directories. 4. Renaissance — Study and teaching (Higher)
Directories. 5. Reformation — Study and teaching (Higher)
Directories. I. Cormack, Lesley B., 1957–　. II. Murray,
Jacqueline, 1953–　. III. Victoria University (Toronto, Ont.).
Centre for Reformation and Renaissance Studies. IV. Title.

CB359.E58　1990　　940.2'072'0025　　C90–093232–5

Contents

Preface 7

Directory 11

Index 65

Preface

The past twenty-five years have seen a blossoming of scholarly research in the Renaissance and Reformation. Societies have been founded at the local, national, and international level to sponsor and encourage such research. Many universities have initiated programmes of study aimed at teaching our youth a multi-disciplinary approach to that period in Western European history that saw itself as a time of 'rebirth' and that led, as Jakob Burckhardt suggested, to the birth of modern Europe. Centres and institutes have been created around special collections, special resources, and special interests to foster particular fields of research within the larger parameters of the Renaissance or the Reformation. Scholarly journals, newsletters, publication and translation series have been founded to meet the needs of scholars to communicate their research and discoveries to each other and to their students.

It is in response to and in honour of exactly such a flowering of research and activity that this Directory was conceived and compiled. It was felt that the time had come to provide colleagues with a clear, compact list of institutional resources available in our field. What societies are there to promote co-operation among scholars of early modern Europe? Where are the physical resources for research? Which journals are available for the dissemination of knowledge and discoveries? Who is organizing seminars, colloquia, conferences at which to present work in progress?

What at first seemed a small task soon revealed itself an Herculean labour. No sooner was one society or centre identified and described than another came to light and had to be located, contacted, and entered into the listing. Eventually, after three years of letters back and forth, we decided to close the golden book and let those who had not yet been included find consolation in the hope of a future re-opening and subsequent edition.

It is with the hope, in fact, of such future editions of this Directory—more comprehensive, more extensive—that we issue the present one. Getting to know each other is an on-going process. As the "Renaissance Meeting '89" held in May 1989 at the Istituto di Studi Rinascimentali (Ferrara) clearly indicated, we are many and we wish to know each other better. One way to do this is to keep in touch and share information about ourselves. This, too, is one of the purposes of the present Directory.

Format of the Directory

The Directory is based on answers to a questionnaire sent out three years ago to a number of associations, centres, and institutes devoted to the study of different aspects of the Renaissance or Reformation. In order to stream-line, as much as possible, the information that was received, the questionnaire format has been retained in the *Directory*, although no such unyielding structure could do justice to the variety inherent in our field and in our work. There are, however, some basic questions about the organizations that need to be asked, such as:

what is its name?

what is its address?

who is in charge?

when was it founded?

how large is the organization?

does it depend on some other agency?

does it have a library?

what does the library specialize in?

is it open to the public?

what does the organization publish?

what are its main focuses of interest?

does it organize seminars, colloquia, conferences?

does it offer courses?

does it offer fellowships?

These, in brief, were the questions we asked. The answers we received have been entered (with a minimal amount of editorial revision) into the *Directory*, either in English or in French, as the respondent preferred. The answer "nil" indicates there is no library/course/fellowship, etc.; the answer "n/a" indicates the respondent did not answer the question.

The Index collects all the names of 14th–17th century persons mentioned in entries, the names of cities where organizations are located, those of journals and other such periodicals, and general subject areas mentioned by the respondents. It also indicates the organizations that offer courses or fellowships.

Abbreviations

The following abbreviations have been used:

Assist.	= Assistant / Assistante
ca.	= circa / about / environs
Dept.	= Department / Département
Dir.	= Director / Directeur
ed.	= editor / éditeur
Exec.	= Executive / Executif
gen.	= general / général
ind.	= independent / indépendent
n/a	= not answered / pas de reponse
p.a.	= per annum / per year / par an
Pres.	= President / Président
Secr.	= Secretary / Secrétaire
tel.	= telephone / téléphone
Treas.	= Treasurer / Trésorier
Univ.	= University / Université

Corrections and suggestions:

We sincerely hope to be able to correct, amend, and improve this *Directory* in future editions, and thus we urge our colleagues to communicate appropriate changes to the compilers at the following address:

Professor Konrad Eisenbichler
Editor, IDRRAI
Victoria College
University of Toronto
Toronto, Canada   M5S 1K7

Acknowledgements

We wish to thank the Centre for Reformation and Renaissance Studies at Victoria University, Toronto (Dr. Germaine Warkentin, Director), the Toronto Renaissance and Reformation Colloquium (Dr. William R. Bowen, Chair), the Renaissance Society of America (Dr. Margaret L. King, Executive Director), and the Istituto di Studi Rinascimentali, Ferrara (dott. Amedeo Quondam, Director) for their enthusiastic support of this project and for their generosity in helping to finance its publication. They share with us the vision of a network of centres, institutes, and societies co-operating to assist scholars working on the Renaissance or Reformation.

We, on the other hand, jealously keep for ourselves the responsibility for the inevitable errors and omissions present in this first edition.

Konrad Eisenbichler
Lesley B. Cormack
Jacqueline Murray

Directory

1. **Accademia Internazionale Burckhardt**
   (Internationale Burckhardt Akademie)
   Piazza San Salvatore in Lauro 13, I-00186 Roma, Italy
   TEL (06) 65–9737 OFFICERS Hon. Pres. Dr. Giovanni di Giuri; Pres. Prof.
   Aurelio Tommaso Prete di Morigerati; Vice-Pres. Dr. Giuseppe Pezzi; Secr. Dr.
   Manlio Cruciani; Dir. Sig. Gianluigi Prete FOUNDED 1946 as a literary centre,
   reconstituted in 1947 as an academy MEMBERSHIP n/a AFFILIATION ind.
   LIBRARY n/a RESEARCH INTERESTS any pursuit which reflects the values
   of the Italian Renaissance as exemplified in Jakob Burckhardt's *The Culture of
   the Renaissance in Italy*. ACTIVITIES lectures, exhibitions, etc. COURSES
   n/a FELLOWSHIPS n/a PUBLICATIONS *La Voce delle Arti e delle Lettere*,
   vol. 1 (monthly journal); *Burckhardt*, vol. 1 (monthly newsletter)

2. **Accademia Raffaello**
   Casa di Raffaello, Via Raffaello 57, I-61029 Urbino, Italy
   TEL 3–7105 OFFICERS Pres. Prof. Francesco Carnevali; Vice-Pres. avv.
   Michelangelo Renzetti; Secr. avv. Nino Baldeschi FOUNDED 1869 MEM-
   BERSHIP n/a AFFILIATION ind. LIBRARY n/a RESEARCH INTERESTS
   Raphael ACTIVITIES the Accademia oversees the Museo and Casa di Raf-
   faello; it holds conferences, colloquia, seminars COURSES n/a FELLOW-
   SHIPS n/a PUBLICATIONS "Collana di Studi e Testi" (series on Raphael and
   on Urbino)

3. **The American Boccaccio Association**
   c/o Romance Languages & Literatures, Washington University, Box 1077, 1
   Brookings Drive, St Louis, MO 63130, USA
   No further information available at this time

4. **American Cusanus Society**
   c/o Prof. Marimichi Watanabe, Long Island University, C.W. Post Campus,
   Greenvale, NY 11548, USA
   No further information available at this time

5. **Amici Thomae Mori**
   c/o Moreanum, Université Catholique de l'Ouest, BP 808, F-49005 Angers Cedex, France
   TEL (41) 88–83–98 OFFICERS Dir. Fr. Germain Marc'hadour (at 29 rue Volney, 49005 Angers) FOUNDED 1963 by the *Amici Thomae Mori* MEMBERSHIP 900 (subscribers to *Moreana*) AFFILIATION part of the IRFA, a research institute within the Univ. Catholique de l'Ouest LIBRARY some 3000 titles; 100 16th-cent. books; 36 journals SPECIALIZATION Thomas More HOURS 6h30–22h ANNUAL CLOSURE nil RESEARCH INTERESTS More's universe and interests ACTIVITIES occasional seminars and colloquia COURSES yes, on the *Utopia* and More's English works; at the B.A., M.A. and predoctoral levels. FELLOWSHIPS one or two students in residence, on a fellowship from the university, help also as research assistants and in the production of *Moreana* PUBLICATIONS *Moreana*, vol. 1 (1963) (4 numbers in 3 yearly issues); Monographs every 2nd year on Erasmus, More, Henry VIII; Newsletter (2 p.a.)

6. **Arbeitsgruppe Renaissanceforschung**
   Freie Universität Berlin, Institut für Romanische Philologien (WE 3), Habelschwerdter Allee 45, 1000 Berlin 33, Germany
   TEL 0039-(0)30–838 20 43 OFFICERS Prof. Dr. Klaus W. Hempfer FOUNDED 1980 AFFILIATION Institut für Romanische Philologien LIBRARY Institute's library SPECIALIZATION Italian Renaissance literature, especially chivalric poetry of the 15th and 16th centuries; lyric poetry from Petrarch to Marino HOURS 9h00–20h00 ANNUAL CLOSURE May RESEARCH INTERESTS chivalric epic poety of the 15th and 16th centuries; lyric poetry from Petrarch to Marino ACTIVITIES colloquia, seminars, conferences COURSES yes, undergraduate and post-graduate FELLOWSHIPS nil PUBLICATIONS staff publications (no independent series or journal)

7. **Arbeitsstelle für Renaissanceforschung**
   Fakultät Sprach- und Literaturwissenschaften, Universität Bamberg, Postfach 1549, An der Universität 5, D-8600 Bamberg, Germany
   TEL (09 51) 863–285 OFFICERS Prof. Dr. Dieter Wuttke (Lehrstuhl für Philologie des Mittelalters und der frühen Neuzeit). No further information available at this time

8. **Archivio Umanistico Rinascimentale Bolognese**
   Bologna, Italy
   No further information available at this time

9. **Arizona Center for Medieval & Renaissance Studies**
   Social Science Bldg 224-B, Arizona State University, Tempe, AZ 85287, USA
   TEL (602) 965–5900 E-MAIL ATJXB@ASUACAD OFFICERS Dir Dr. Jean R. Brink FOUNDED 1981 MEMBERSHIP n/a AFFILIATION Arizona State

University LIBRARY the University Library includes the libraries of Robert Lopez and William R. Ringler (Shakespeare collection) RESEARCH INTERESTS all aspects of medieval and Renaissance culture, from 400 to 1700 AD. Special support of history of science and technology. ACTIVITIES Autumn and Spring lecture series; occasional national conferences. COURSES nil FELLOWSHIPS post-doctoral fellowships for young scholars; Visiting Scholar Program; Visiting Professor Program (in conjunction with the Univ. of Arizona and Northern Arizona University; nominated by local faculty) PUBLICATIONS edited collection of essays now in progress

10. **The Armand Hammer Center for Leonardo Studies**
    c/o University of California, Los Angeles, CA 90024, USA
    No further information available at this time

11. **Association d'Etude sur l'Humanisme, la Réforme, et la Renaissance**
    4 av. Adolphe Max, F-69005 Lyon, France
    TEL n/a OFFICERS Dir. Prof. Henri Weber; Conseil d'administration de 19 membres FOUNDED 1975 MEMBERSHIP 250 AFFILIATION ind. LIBRARY nil RESEARCH INTERESTS langues, littérature et civilisation de la France et des pays voisins du 15e au 17e siècle. ACTIVITIES colloque bisannuel. COURSES n/a FELLOWSHIPS n/a PUBLICATIONS *Bulletin Réforme, Humanisme, Renaissance*, vol. 1 (1975) (2 p.a.); Actes des colloques

12. **Association Humanisme et Renaissance**
    c/o Librairie Droz S.A., 11 rue Massot, CH-1211 Genève 12, Switzerland
    TEL 46–6666 OFFICERS Secr. Prof. Alain Dufour FOUNDED 1933 MEMBERSHIP Members are subscribers of BHR AFFILIATION ind. LIBRARY nil RESEARCH INTERESTS XVe-XVIe siècles ACTIVITIES publication de la revue COURSES nil FELLOWSHIPS nil PUBLICATIONS *Bibliothèque d'Humanisme et Renaissance* Vol. 1 (1965); *Nouvelle Revue du Seizième Siècle*, vol. 1 (1983) (annual)

13. **Association Internationale des Historiens de la Renaissance**
    Paris, France
    OFFICERS Prof. R. Marcel. No further information available at this time

14. **Australia and New Zealand Association for Medieval and Renaissance Studies**
    The Editor, *Parergon*, Dept of English, University of Sydney, Sydney, NSW 2006, Australia
    Tel (02) 692–3251 (Dept of English) OFFICERS Editorial Committee of *Parergon* Conal Condren, Geraldine Barnes, Elizabeth Jeffreys, and six others. A new committee will be appointed in January 1990. MEMBERSHIP 250 paid members AFFILIATION independent LIBRARY nil RESEARCH INTERESTS Medieval and Renaissance studies COURSES nil FELLOWSHIPS nil PUBLICATIONS *Parergon* (annual)

15. **Barnabe Riche Society**
Department of English, 1812 Dunton Tower, Carleton University, Ottawa, Ontario, Canada K1S 5B6
TEL (613)-564–6715 OFFICERS Dir. Douglas Wurtele; Series Eds. Faith Gildenhuys and Donald Beecher FOUNDED 1988 by Donald Beecher MEMBERSHIP Granted upon completion & publication of a text in the series AFFILIATION ind. LIBRARY nil RESEARCH INTERESTS Goal is to publish English Renaissance prose fiction and non-fiction in editions with scholarly introductions and notes ACTIVITIES Colloquia and conferences planned COURSES nil FELLOWSHIPS nil PUBLICATIONS 6 forthcoming (1989–90)

16. **Biblioteca Hertziana Max Planck Institut**
Via Gregoriana 28, I-00187 Roma, Italy
TEL 679–7352 OFFICERS Pres. Prof. Reimar Lüst; Dir. Prof. Christoph Luitpold Frommel, Prof. Mattias Winner FOUNDED 1913 MEMBERSHIP n/a AFFILIATION Max Planck Institute (headquarters Residenzstrasse 1a, Munich, West Germany) LIBRARY 150,000 vols.; fototeca of 300,000 photographs, 18,000 negatives, 9,000 slides SPECIALIZATION Italian art from the Middle Ages to the 20th cent. HOURS n/a ANNUAL CLOSURE n/a RESEARCH INTERESTS Italian art ACTIVITIES conferences, seminars, colloquia PUBLICATIONS *Römisches Jahrbuch für Kunstgeschichte*, vol. 1 (1937) . . . vol. 23/24 (1988) (annual journal)

17. **Borthwick Institute of Historical Research**
St Anthony's Hall, Peasholme Green, York YO1 2PW, England
TEL (0904) 43–0000, ext. 274 or (0904) 642315 OFFICERS Dir. Dr. D.M. Smith FOUNDED 1953 MEMBERSHIP n/a AFFILIATION Univ. of York LIBRARY Gurney Library 20,000 vols; archives of the diocese of York and Northern Province. SPECIALIZATION ecclesiastical, social and economic history. HOURS 9h30–1h00, 2h00–5h00, Monday to Friday; by appointment ANNUAL CLOSURE short periods at Christmas and Easter; bank holidays RESEARCH INTERESTS from medieval episcopal and monastic history to early modern religious and social history. ACTIVITIES occasional conferences, seminars, and colloquia. COURSES palaeography 1200–1600 (a four-day course for postgraduate students each Christmas) FELLOWSHIPS non-stipendiary visiting fellowship in history. EXTRACT FROM BROCHURE The records of the archbishopric of York date from the pontificate of Walter de Gray (1215–1255). The Institute also has custody of the Church Commissioners' records for the secular estates of the diocese of York; the probate records of the diocese; the archives from Bishopthorpe Palace; parish records. Fuller details can be found in *Guide to the Archive Collections in the Borthwick Institute of Historical Research* (1973), and a *Supplementary Guide* (1980), both published by the Institute. For genealogical enquiries there is the *Guide to Genealogical Sources at the Borthwick Institute* (1981) PUBLICATIONS *Borthwick Institute Bulletin*;

Borthwick Texts and Calendars (editions, calendars and handlists); Borthwick Wallets (guides to the handwriting and content of the records); Borthwick Papers (studies concerned with the ecclesiastical history of the north of England)

18. **Bucer Institut**
Münster, Germany
Dir. Robert Stupperich PUBLICATIONS *Martin Bucers Deutsche Schriften.* No further information available at this time

19. **Canadian Society for the History of Rhetoric**
c/o Prof. Albert W. Halsau, Dept of French, Carleton University, Ottawa, Canada K1S 5B6
TEL (613) 564–3854 OFFICERS Pres. Prof. Albert W. Halsau (see above for address); Secr.-Treasurer Prof. Nan Johnson (Dept of English, Univ. of British Columbia) FOUNDED n/a MEMBERSHIP n/a AFFILIATION ind. LIBRARY nil RESEARCH INTERESTS rhetoric; theory and practice from 6th cent. BC to 20th cent. AD ACTIVITIES occasional lecture; annual meeting COURSES nil FELLOWSHIPS nil PUBLICATIONS "Canadian Rhetoric Newsletter" vol. 1 (1986) (2 p.a.)

20. **Canadian Society for Renaissance Studies**
c/o Dept of History, Queen's University, Kingston, Ontario, Canada K7L 3N6 TEL (416) 585–4484 OFFICERS Pres. Prof. François Paré; Vice-Pres. Prof. Anthony Raspa; Secr.-Treasurer Prof. Lesley Cormack FOUNDED 1976 MEMBERSHIP ca. 200 AFFILIATION ind. society LIBRARY nil RESEARCH INTERESTS all areas of Renaissance studies ACTIVITIES annual national conference in May; occasionally sponsors regional conferences COURSES nil FELLOWSHIPS nil PUBLICATIONS "Newsletter/Bulletin", vol. 1 (3 issues p.a.); *Directory/Repertoire* (directory of Canadian Renaissance scholars); *Renaissance and Reformation/Renaissance et Réforme* (journal vol. 1, 1964)

21. **Center for Medieval and Early Renaissance Studies**
State University of New York, Binghamton, NY 13901, USA
TEL (607) 777–2730 E-MAIL (for Mario Di Cesare and MRTS) BG0344@BINGVMA OFFICERS Dir. Prof. Paul E. Szarmach FOUNDED 1966 MEMBERSHIP n/a AFFILIATION SUNY-Binghamton LIBRARY n/a RESEARCH INTERESTS interdisciplinary study of the 5th to 17th centuries ACTIVITIES annual conference in October; "Renaissance Bibliographical Resources" (project) COURSES towards a B.A., and also towards graduate certification FELLOWSHIPS n/a PUBLICATIONS *Acta*, vol. 1 (annual); *Mediaevalia*, vol. 1 (annual); "Medieval & Renaissance Texts & Studies" (series); and "Pegasus Paperbooks" (series); "Old English Newsletter", vol. 1 (2 p.a.)

22. **Center for Medieval and Renaissance Studies**
212 Royce Hall, University of California, 405 Hilgard Ave., Los Angeles, CA 90024, USA

TEL (213) 825–1880 OFFICERS Dir. Fredi Chiappelli; Assoc. Dir. Michael J.B. Allen FOUNDED 1963 MEMBERSHIP approximately 120 faculty members and 60 families in Community Support Group. AFFILIATION Univ. of California at Los Angeles LIBRARY small faculty library; access to UCLA library (5,000,000 vols) SPECIALIZATION interdisciplinary in medieval and Renaissance field HOURS 8h00–17h00 ANNUAL CLOSURE nil RESEARCH INTERESTS all aspects of the Middle Ages and the Renaissance ACTIVITIES conferences, colloquia, seminars, research COURSES nil FELLOWSHIPS Research Associates; Research Assistantships, Summer Fellowships, Visiting Professors; Visiting Scholars, Postdoctoral Scholars, Lynn White Fellowship PUBLICATIONS *Viator*, vol. 1 (1970) (annual journal); *Comitatus*, vol. 1 (1970) (annual); assorted publications through the Univ. of California Press and Peter Lang Publishers

23. **Center for Medieval and Renaissance Studies**
Department of English, Duke University, Durham, NC 27706, USA
TEL 919–684–2741 OFFICERS Chairman Lee Patterson; Dir. Grad. Studies Charles Young; Dir. Undergrad. Studies Ronald Witt FOUNDED 1960 MEMBERSHIP n/a AFFILIATION Duke University LIBRARY n/a RESEARCH INTERESTS n/a ACTIVITIES lecture series, colloquia COURSES both undergraduate majors and graduate programs FELLOWSHIPS fellowship support is provided for graduate students PUBLICATIONS *Journal of Medieval and Renaissance Studies*; monographs in Medieval and Renaissance Studies

24. **Center for Medieval and Renaissance Studies**
Ohio State University, 322 Dulles Hall, 230 West 17th Avenue, Columbus, OH 43210–1311, USA
TEL (614) 292–7495 OFFICERS Dir. Prof. Christian K. Zacher FOUNDED 1965 MEMBERSHIP n/a AFFILIATION Ohio State Univ. LIBRARY nil RESEARCH INTERESTS CMRS supports and encourages the research of approximately 100 faculty affiliates whose combined interests encompass most areas of medieval and Renaissance studies. ACTIVITIES graduate seminars on special topics, annual conferences on selected topics in February, colloquia. COURSES leading to a B.A. in Medieval and Renaissance Studies. FELLOWSHIPS nil PUBLICATIONS "Nouvelles Nouvelles", vol. 1 (Newsletter, 3 p.a.); occasional proceedings

25. **Center for Medieval and Renaissance Studies**
University of Pittsburgh, Dept of French, Pittsburgh, PA 15260, USA
OFFICERS Dir. Prof. Daniel Russel. No further information available at this time

26. **Center for Medieval Studies**
    Fordham University, Fordham Road, Bronx, NY 10458, USA
    OFFICERS Dir. Prof. Thelma Fenster. No further information available at this time

27. **Center for Reformation Research**
    6477 San Bonita Avenue, St Louis, MO 63105, USA
    TEL (314) 727–6655 OFFICERS Pres. Prof. Robert M. Kingdon (Univ. of Wisconsin-Madison); Exec. Dir. Prof. William S. Maltby FOUNDED 1957 MEMBERSHIP n/a AFFILIATION ind. LIBRARY 2500 modern imprints; 12,000 microfilms (= 500,000 mss) SPECIALIZATION history of the Protestant Reformation HOURS 8h30–15h00 Monday, Wednesday, Friday, and by appointment ANNUAL CLOSURE nil RESEARCH INTERESTS history of the Protestant Reformation ACTIVITIES conferences, seminars, colloquia COURSES nil FELLOWSHIPS Summer Paleography Institute Fellowships for graduate students. PUBLICATIONS "Sixteenth Century Bibliography" (series); "CRR Newsletter", vol. 1; guides to research

28. **Center for Renaissance and Baroque Studies**
    Francis Scott Key Hall, University of Maryland, College Park, MD 20742, USA
    TEL (301) 454–2740 OFFICERS Dir. (1987) S. Schoenbaum; Exec. Dir. Adele Seeff FOUNDED 1981 MEMBERSHIP n/a AFFILIATION Univ. of Maryland LIBRARY n/a RESEARCH INTERESTS arts and humanities, history and philosophy of science, history of law ACTIVITIES n/a COURSES n/a FELLOWSHIPS n/a PUBLICATIONS n/a

29. **Center for Renaissance Studies**
    The Newberry Library, 60 West Walton Street, Chicago, IL 60610, USA
    TEL (312) 943–9090 OFFICERS Dir. Dr. Mary Beth Rose; Admin. Assist. Mary Pat Mauro FOUNDED 1979 MEMBERSHIP 24 universities in the Midwest form the consortium of the Center AFFILIATION The Newberry Library LIBRARY ca. 1,400,000 vols. (ca 200 pre-1500 European mss; ca. 1,000,000 other mss; 250,000 vols in Special Collections; 2000+ incunabula; 242,000 microforms; 1000 journals) SPECIALIZATION European History and Culture, esp. literature, theology, history of education, history of the book, contact between Europe and the New World HOURS 10h00–18h00, Tues.-Thurs.; 9h00–17h00 Fri.; 9h00–17h00 Sat. ANNUAL CLOSURE Sundays, Mondays, and all national holidays RESEARCH INTERESTS to encourage interdisciplinary research and work with primary sources in the Middle Ages and Renaissance; subject areas include literature, history, and the humanities in England and on the Continent. ACTIVITIES postdoctoral seminars funded by NEH; one/two day workshops on interdisciplinary research and bibliography; an annual Renaissance conference, summer institutes, usually in paleography. COURSES faculty from 24 Midwestern universities in the Newberry Library Center for

Renaissance Studies Consortium offer graduate courses at the Library at the graduate and postdoctoral level. FELLOWSHIPS through the NEH the Center offers stipends for faculty in U.S. institutions to attend the Summer Institutes in Paleography. The Consortium schools have funds for their faculty and graduate students to participate in the programs or do research at the Newberry. PUBLICATIONS *Corpus Reformatorum Italicorum* (co-publisher) *Renaissance Drama*, n.s. vol. 1 (1968) (annual) M.B. Rose, current editor; "Newsletter" (2 p.a.)

30. **Center for Renaissance Studies**
    317 17th Ave. S.E., Minneapolis, MN 55414, USA
    TEL (612) 379–4463 OFFICERS Dir. Dr. Arthur Maud FOUNDED 1966 MEMBERSHIP n/a AFFILIATION n/a LIBRARY 2000 vols. SPECIALIZA-TION Renaissance music and dance sources HOURS contact Mark R. Ellenberger, administrator ANNUAL CLOSURE n/a RESEARCH INTERESTS Music and dance of the Middle Ages and the Renaissance; affiliated with the performance group "Concentus Musicus" ACTIVITIES n/a COURSES n/a FELLOWSHIPS n/a PUBLICATIONS n/a

31. **Center for Study of Renaissance and Baroque Arts**
    Pennsylvania State University, 226 Arts II Building, University Park, PA 16802, USA
    TEL (814) 865–6326 OFFICERS Head Dr. Hellmut Hager FOUNDED 1966 MEMBERSHIP n/a AFFILIATION Penn. State Univ. LIBRARY 500 vols., slides, photographs SPECIALIZATION art and architectural history HOURS n/a ANNUAL CLOSURE n/a RESEARCH INTERESTS art historical studies, esp. of the Italian Renaissance and Baroque; Dutch Painting in the Age of Rembrandt; architecture ACTIVITIES annual lecture series on changing areas of concentration. COURSES Graduate and undergraduate courses in Italian and Northern Renaissance and Baroque Art and Architecture FELLOWSHIPS Francis Hyslop Memorial Fellowship PUBLICATIONS n/a

32. **Central Renaissance Conference**
    c/o Dept of English, 231 Arts and Science, University of Missouri, Columbia, MO 65211, USA
    TEL (314) 882–3525 OFFICERS Exec. Secr. John R. Roberts (Missouri) FOUNDED n/a MEMBERSHIP n/a AFFILIATION Renaissance Society of America LIBRARY nil RESEARCH INTERESTS English, history, art history, music, French, Italian, German any topic related to the Renaissance. ACTIVI-TIES an annual conference in March or April COURSES nil FELLOWSHIPS nil PUBLICATIONS nil

33. **Centre de Recherches de la Renaissance**
    Ménesi út 11–13, 1118 Budapest IX, Hongrie
    TEL 36/1/669–643 OFFICERS Dir. Tibor Klaniczay (1970–); Dir. ad-

joint Iván Horváth (1983–) FOUNDED 1970, par Inst. d'Etudes Littér., Acad. Hongroise des Sciences MEMBERSHIP équipe permanente (salariée) de 9 chercheurs; membres adhérants 170 (sans côtisation) AFFILIATION Institut d'Etudes Littéraires, Acad. Hongroise des Sciences LIBRARY 7,000 livres anciens, 140,000 imprimés modernes, 250 périodiques SPECIALIZATION histoire, littérature, civilisation hongroises HOURS 9–17h, lundi à vendredi ANNUAL CLOSURE août RESEARCH INTERESTS Humanisme, Renaissance, Réforme en Hongrie; éditions des textes latins et hongrois des XVe et XVIe siècles; histoire comparée des littératures de la Renaissance. ACTIVITIES colloques annuels et occasionnels. COURSES nil FELLOWSHIPS accueil des boursiers hongrois et étrangers PUBLICATIONS *Studia Humanitatis*, vol. 1 (1973); *Humanizmus és Reformáció*, vol. 1 (1973) (Humanisme et Réforme. Travaux individuels sur la Renaissance en Hongrie, publiés en hongrois); *Memoria Saeculorum Hungariae*, vol. 1 (1974); *Bibliotheca Scriptorum Medii Recentisque Aevorum* s.n. vol. 1 (1976) (Editions critiques des textes néolatins); *Régi Magyar Költok Tára* vol. 1 (1959) (Collection des Anciens Poètes Hongrois; XVIe et XVII siècles); *Bibliotheca Hungarica Antiqua* vol. 1 (1960) (fac-similés d'anciens imprimés hongrois, accompagnés d'une étude); *Bibliotheca Unitariorum* vol. 1 (1983) (fac-similés d'anciens imprimés antitrinitaires, accompagnés d'une étude en anglais)

34. **Centre de Recherches Pré-Renaissance, Humanisme et Baroque**
Université Stendhal, BP 25, F-38040 Grenoble Cedex, France
TEL 00–33 76 44–8218, poste 3323 OFFICERS Dir. Prof. J. Chocheyras (1983–); Dir.-adjoint Prof. J. Serroy (1985–) FOUNDED par Prof. Charles Béné MEMBERSHIP n/a AFFILIATION Université Stendhal LIBRARY oui SPECIALIZATION Dialectologie franco-provensale et occitane HOURS 8h30–17h30 ANNUAL CLOSURE 30 juin 15 septembre RESEARCH INTERESTS traductions; Erasmus; théâtre religieux; poésie baroque; vies de saints. ACTIVITIES séminaires occasionnels COURSES oui, sur tous sujets de recherche; Maîtrise, DEA, Doctorat FELLOWSHIPS non, mais assistance des rechercheurs étrangers PUBLICATIONS textes et éditions critiques

35. **Centre de Recherche sur l'Espagne des XVIe et XVIIe Siècles**
rue Gay-Lussac 31, F-75005 Paris, France
OFFICERS Dir. Prof. A. Redondo. No further information available at this time

36. **Centre de Recherche sur l'Histoire Sociale et Culturelle de l'Occident XIIe-XVIIIe Siècle**
Université de Paris X, Paris, France
TEL (1) 40–97–75–73 OFFICERS Pres. Prof. Hugues Neveu (Histoire moderne); Vice-Pres. André Vauchez (Histoire du Moyen Age) FOUNDED 1984 (par le Prof. Philippe Contamine) MEMBERSHIP tous les enseignants-chercheurs de l'Université de Paris X; spécialistes d'histoire médiévale et mod-

erne. AFFILIATION Faculté "Sciences Sociales d'Aministrations", Université de Paris X, Nanterre. LIBRARY non RESEARCH INTERESTS le prophétisme en Occident, XIIe-XVIe; histoire de la guerre et de la paix au Moyen Age. ACTIVITIES 1 table ronde en 1988 (programme ajoint) COURSES 3 séminaires de recherche FELLOWSHIPS n/a PUBLICATIONS nil

37. **Centre de Recherches Interdisciplinaires sur la Renaissance**
Rue Madame 41, F-75006 Paris, France
OFFICERS M.-T. Jones-Davies (1985). No further information available at this time

38. **Centre de Recherches Médievales et Néohelléniques**
rue Anagnostopoulou 14, 106 73 Athènes, Grèce
TEL (01)-3623404 OFFICERS Dir. D. Z. Sofianos FOUNDED 1929 MEMBERSHIP 8 AFFILIATION Académie d'Athènes LIBRARY 9,000 vols. SPECIALIZATION Histoire et littérature post-byzantines HOURS 10h00–13h00 tous les jours; pour l'admission contacter le directeur ANNUAL CLOSURE nil RESEARCH INTERESTS histoire et littérature post-byzantines. ACTIVITIES nil COURSES nil FELLOWSHIPS nil PUBLICATIONS *Messaionika kai nea Hellenika* (périodique); *Les Manuscrits de Météores* (catalogue descriptifs); travaux

39. **Centre de Recherches sur la Littérature du Moyen Age et de la Renaissance**
57 rue Pierre Taistinger, F-51100 Reims, France
TEL (26) 08–2323 poste 698 ou 697 OFFICERS Pres. Prof. Yvonne Bellenger (1988); Secr. Georges Forestier (1988); Treas. Danielle Quéruel (1988) FOUNDED 1984 MEMBERSHIP gratuit AFFILIATION Univ. de Reims LIBRARY oui, mais confiée et consultable à la bibl. univ. voisine SPECIALIZATION littérature du Moyen Age et de la Renaissance HOURS voir Bibl. Univ. Reims, av. François Mauriac, 51100 Reims ANNUAL CLOSURE des vacances d'été RESEARCH INTERESTS littérature du Moyen Age et de la Renaissance; problèmes de la référence; region la Champagne (production littéraire); relations Orient-Occident. ACTIVITIES seminaires et colloques annuels COURSES nil FELLOWSHIPS nil; assistance intellectuel PUBLICATIONS *Etudes Champenoises*, vol. 5 (1986); actes de colloques; quelques traductions; communications

40. **Centre de Recherche sur l'Italie à l'époque de la Réforme et la Contre-Réforme (C.R.I.R.C.)**
Paris 3, France
TEL n/a OFFICERS Adelire Fiorato FOUNDED 1981 AFFILIATION affilié avec le Regroupement de Recherche sur les Problèmes de la Modernité (XVe-XVIIe) Français-Italien-Espagnol RESEARCH INTERESTS Etudes des rapports entre la culture au sens le plus large et les structures de l'organisation

politique et sociale ACTIVITIES un seminaire mensuel; un colloque chaque 2 ou 3 années PUBLICATIONS Cahiers de la Renaissance Italienne (2 vols to date, 1987 & 1989)

41. **Centre d'Etudes de la Renaissance**
Université de Sherbrooke, 2500 blvd de l'Université, Sherbrooke, Québec, Canada J1K 2R1
TEL (819) 821–7185 OFFICERS Dir. Prof. J. Martinez De Bujanda FOUNDED n/a MEMBERSHIP n/a AFFILIATION Université de Sherbrooke LIBRARY 5000 vols et microfilms SPECIALIZATION histoire culturelle de la Renaissance RESEARCH INTERESTS Renaissance, histoire intellectuelle, censure. ACTIVITIES editions, enseignement, conférences, séminaires. COURSES oui FELLOWSHIPS nil PUBLICATIONS *Index des livres interdits* (5 vols); "Collection du Centre d'Etudes de la Renaissance" (11 vols)

42. **Centre d'Etudes et de Recherches Elisabéthaines**
Université Paul Valéry, Route de Mende B.P. 5043, 34032 Montpellier, France TEL 67–84–03–54, ext.   427 OFFICERS n/a FOUNDED 1972 par Antione Demadre MEMBERSHIP n/a AFFILIATION n/a LIBRARY Bibliotheque du C.E.R.E., approx. 5,000 vols. HOURS 9h00–12h00, 14h00–17h00 ANNUAL CLOSURE 14 juillet-15 septembre, 18 decembre-5 janv ier, Pâques COURSES Courses on Shakespeare for undergraduate, graduate, post-graduate students FELLOWSHIPS nil PUBLICATIONS *Cahiers Elisabéthains*, vol. 1 (1972) (semi-annuel); *Astraea* (Collections) special editions. Vol. 1 *All's Well That Ends Well Nouvelles Perspectives Critiques* (Montpelier, 1980)

43. **Centre d'Etudes Supérieures de la Renaissance**
59 rue Nericault Destouche, BP 1328, F-37013 Tours, France
TEL (47) 20–7186 OFFICERS Dir. Prof. Robert Sauzet; Dir. adjoint Prof. Pierre Aquilon FOUNDED 1956 MEMBERSHIP n/a AFFILIATION Univ. de Tours LIBRARY 34,850 vols.; 3000 livres anciens; 20 périodiques HOURS 9–12h30, 13h30–17h, lundi au vendredi ANNUAL CLOSURE 17 juillet au 15 août RESEARCH INTERESTS philosophie de la Renaissance; histoire de l'architecture; histoire religieuse; littérature française XVIe; théâtre anglais, XVIe; musicologie. ACTIVITIES colloque international annuel (2 semaines); séminaires du groupe de recherche (4 par an); colloque annuel d'Histoire de l'architecture; tables rondes, colloques divers. COURSES au niveau de Maîtrise, D.E.A., Doctorat.   FELLOWSHIPS accord de co-opération avec Barnard College (Columbia Univ.), NY PUBLICATIONS "De Pétraque à Descartes" (Vrin); "Textes et Documents" (Vrin); "L'oiseau de Minerve" (Vrin); "De Architectura" (Picard)

44. **Centre d'Histoire des Réformes et du Protestantisme**
Université de Montpellier III, B.P. 5043, F-34032 Montpellier, France
OFFICERS Dir. (1985) Michel Peronnet. No further information available at
this time

45. **Centre Européen d'Histoire de la Médecine**
Université Louis Pasteur, 4 rue Blaise Pascal, F-67070 Strasbourg, France
No further information available at this time

46. **Centre for Medieval Studies**
39 Queen's Park Crescent East, University of Toronto, Toronto, Ontario,
Canada M5S 1A1
TEL (416) 978–4884 OFFICERS Dir. (1989-) Prof. Jill Webster; Associate Dir.
Prof. Roberta Frank; Graduate Co-ordinator Prof. Frank Collins FOUNDED
1964 MEMBERSHIP ca.   500, including alumni AFFILIATION Univ. of
Toronto LIBRARY access to the library of the Pontifical Institute for Medieval
Studies (76,500 vols); and to the Univ. of Toronto libraries SPECIALIZA-
TION paleography, philosophy, theology, literature, history, art history, Slavic
studies, musicology, Medieval Latin and vernacular languages HOURS 9–5h;
admission with pass issued by Chief Librarian of the PIMS ANNUAL CLO-
SURE nil RESEARCH INTERESTS all aspects of European Medieval history
and culture, including Byzantine and Slavic. ACTIVITIES annual conference;
occasional international conferences and colloquia; annual Saturday symposium
(with Continuing Studies); annual Bertie Wilkinson Memorial Lecture; annual
Open House (U of T Day) COURSES yes, towards M.A., Ph.D. FELLOW-
SHIPS for graduate students through the School of Graduate Studies at the
Univ. of Toronto; PIMS has some stipendiary and non-stipendiary scholars; the
Centre has some non-stipendiary visiting scholars PUBLICATIONS *Mediaeval
Studies*, vol. 1 (1939) (published by the PIMS); *Scintilla*, vol. 1 (1984) (publ. by
the grad. students at the Centre); "Newsletter", vol. 1 (1984) (published twice
yearly); "Toronto Medieval Latin Texts"; "Toronto Medieval Texts and Transla-
tions"; "Toronto Old English Series"; "Toronto Medieval Bibliographies"; *Old
English Dictionary*; *Records of Early English Drama*

47. **Centre for Medieval Studies**
Emmanuel Institute, University of Leeds, Leeds LS2 9JT, United Kingdom
TEL (0532 Leeds) 43–1751 OFFICERS Dir. (1988–1993) Dr. L.A.S. Butler
FOUNDED 1967 MEMBERSHIP Medievalists within the University of Leeds
AFFILIATION Univ. of Leeds LIBRARY nil RESEARCH INTERESTS Me-
dieval European Drama; areas of interest particular to the individual mem-
bers. ACTIVITIES occasional conferences; reconstructions of theatrical per-
formances COURSES yes, at the M.A. level FELLOWSHIPS nil PUBLICA-
TIONS "Leeds Medieval Studies" (occasional monograph series)

48. **Centre for Medieval Studies**
    The King's Manor, University of York, Heslington, York YO1 2EP, England
    TEL (0904) 43–0000 OFFICERS Co-directors Prof. Martin Carver (Archae-
    ology), Prof. Alastair Minnis (English) FOUNDED n/a MEMBERSHIP n/a
    AFFILIATION Univ. of York LIBRARY The Wormald Library (affiliated with
    the Univ. of York Library) SPECIALIZATION Anglo-Saxon archaeology and
    literature; medieval authorship; history of York and the ecclesiastical province
    of York. HOURS 9h00–21h00; access obtained by writing to the Secretary, The
    Centre for Medieval Studies. ANNUAL CLOSURE nil RESEARCH INTER-
    ESTS see above. Also the late medieval city; Cistercian art and architecture;
    medieval English monasticism; the English Reformation (esp. in the north of
    England). ACTIVITIES colloquia on medieval and Renaissance manuscripts
    every two years. COURSES yes, towards an M.A. in Medieval Studies (20
    students per year) and a D. Phil. FELLOWSHIPS nil, but non-stipendiary Vis-
    iting Fellowships can be arranged with the Archaeology, History, or English
    departments PUBLICATIONS occasional proceedings of conferences held at
    the Centre

49. **Centre for Reformation and Renaissance Studies**
    Victoria University, University of Toronto, Toronto, Ontario, Canada M5S 1K7
    TEL (416) 585–4484 or 585–4468 FAX (416) 585–4584 OFFICERS Dir. Prof.
    Germaine Warkentin; Curator Dr. Jacqueline Glomski FOUNDED 1964 MEM-
    BERSHIP n/a AFFILIATION Victoria Univ. in the Univ. of Toronto LIBRARY
    4000 rare books; 17,000 modern imprints; microfilms. SPECIALIZATION ex-
    tensive collection of 16th Century ed. of Erasmus' works, England, France,
    Swiss Reformation HOURS 9h00–17h00 Mon. to Fri. ANNUAL CLOSURE
    August, Christmas to New Year RESEARCH INTERESTS Erasmus, Zwingli,
    Calvin, Bucer, Northern European Renaissance (England, France, Germany,
    Switzerland), Italian Humanism, Swiss and German Reformation. ACTIVI-
    TIES lectures, conferences, colloquia, annual series of seminars; annual Eras-
    mus Lecture; annual Distinguished Visiting Scholar Programme; co-operation
    with the Toronto Renaissance and Reformation Colloquium (q.v.). COURSES
    nil (but assists the Renaissance Studies Programme at the University, leading
    to a B.A. with a Major in Renaissance Studies) FELLOWSHIPS two Grad-
    uate Fellowships (stipendiary); non-stipendiary Senior Fellowships (for post-
    doctoral research). PUBLICATIONS *Renaissance and Reformation / Renais-
    sance et Réforme*, vol. 1 (1964) (4 p.a.); "Newsletter", vol. 1 (1982) (6 p.a.);
    "Renaissance and Reformation Texts in Translation" (series; 4 titles to date);
    "Occasional Publications" (series; 6 titles to date)

50. **Centre for Renaissance Studies**
    c/o Prof. Brian Vickers, ETH-Zentrum, Rämistrasse 101, CH-8092 Zürich,
    Switzerland
    TEL (01) 256–4004 OFFICERS Dir. Prof. Brian Vickers FOUNDED 1976;

'birthplace' of International Society for the History of Rhetoric (founded 1977) MEMBERSHIP n/a AFFILIATION Eidgenössische Technische Hochschule (= Ecole Polytechnique Fédérale) LIBRARY yes; small reference library; major Renaissance journals RESEARCH INTERESTS Rhetoric, Philosophy, History of Science, History of Literature. ACTIVITIES Conferences (intermittently) on Renaissance topics, followed by publication of papers. Next symposium "Moral Philosophy in the Renaissance". COURSES nil FELLOWSHIPS nil PUBLI-CATIONS Vickers, Brian, ed. *Rhetoric Revalued. Papers from the International Society for the History of Rhetoric* (Binghamton, 1982); *Occult and Scientific Mentalities in the Renaissance* (Cambridge, 1984); *Arbeit, Musse, Meditation. Betrachtungen zur Vita activa und Vita contemplativa* (Zürich, 1985)

51. **Centre Interuniversitaire de Recherche sur la Renaissance Italienne (C.I.R.R.I.)**
13 rue de Santeuil ,Université de la Sorbonne Nouvelle, F-75231 Paris Cedex 5, France
TEL 1–45–87–41–41 OFFICERS José Guidi (1989); Marina Marietti (1990) FOUNDED 1969 AFFILIATION unité de recherche associée au CNRS RE-SEARCH INTERESTS Renaissance Italian literature ACTIVITES seminaires mensuels, un colloque pour le novembre 1990 COURSES Diplôme d'Etudes Approfondies FELLOWSHIPS n/a PUBLICATIONS textes et études, un volume chaque année (16 vols)

52. **Centre V.L. Saulnier de Recherche sur la Création Littéraire en France au XVIe siècle**
rue Victor Cousin 1, F-75230 Paris Cedex 05, France
TEL (1) 40–46–26–54 OFFICERS Prof. Robert Aulotte; Prof. Jacques Bailbé FOUNDED 1982 MEMBERSHIP n/a AFFILIATION Université de Paris Sorbonne LIBRARY nil RESEARCH INTERESTS littérature polémique en France au XVIe siècle ACTIVITIES séminaires durant l'année universitaire; colloque international annuel (mi-mars); "Jeudis V.L. Saulnier" le 1er jeudi de chaque mois. COURSES dans le cadre de l'université FELLOWSHIPS nil PUBLICA-TIONS *Cahiers V.L. Saulnier*, vol. 1

53. **Centro di Studi del Pensiero Filosofico del Cinque-Seicento**
c/o Istituto di Storia della Filosofia, Facoltà di Lettere e Filosofia, Università degli Studi, Via Albricci 9, I-20122 Milano, Italy
TEL 805–2538 OFFICERS Dir. Prof. Mario Dal Pra FOUNDED 1971 MEM-BERSHIP n/a AFFILIATION Università degli Studi, Milano LIBRARY access to the university library RESEARCH INTERESTS the systematic study of philosophic thought in the 16th and 17th century with respect to the history of science PUBLICATIONS n/a

54. **Centro di Studi Medievali e Umanistici**
Perugia, Italy
No further information available at this time

55. **Centro di Studi per la Storia del Teatro Italiano (CSSTI)**
Istituto Nazionale di Studi sul Rinascimento, Piazza Strozzi, Palazzo Strozzi,
I-50123 Firenze, Italy
TEL (055) 28.77.28 OFFICERS Coordinator CSSTI Dott. Elvira Garbero
Zorzi; Pres. Istituto Naz. (see Affilation) Prof. Eugenio Garin FOUNDED
1980 MEMBERSHIP n/a AFFILIATION CSSTI is a library section of Istituto
Nazionale di Studi sul Rinascimento LIBRARY yes; 2,500 books; 15 jour-
nal subscriptions; 50 microfilms SPECIALIZATION History of Italian Renais-
sance theatre, civilization HOURS 9h00–13h00 Monday Saturday ANNUAL
CLOSURE August RESEARCH INTERESTS Feasts; 'Commedia dell'Arte';
Theatrical Italian architecture ACTIVITIES occasional seminars and confer-
ences COURSES nil FELLOWSHIPS The CSSTI assists outside researchers
PUBLICATIONS n/a

56. **Centro di Studi Sorani "Vincenzo Patriarca"**
Via Emilio Zincone, 14, Casella Postale n. 121, I-03039 Sora (Frosinone), Italy
TEL (0776) 83.37.93 OFFICERS Pres. & Founder Prof. Dr. Luigi Gulia
FOUNDED 1977 MEMBERSHIP 135 AFFILIATION ind. LIBRARY in-house
library, ca 2,000 vols.; affiliated with other specialized libraries and archives
SPECIALIZATION history and culture of Southern Latium HOURS 16h00–
20h00 ANNUAL CLOSURE August RESEARCH INTERESTS the contribu-
tion of humanists from the Latium region to humanism; card. Cesare Baronio
(Sorano); Counter-Reformation ACTIVITIES to catalogue and appraise the local patrimony, esp. with respect to the dialect of the Ciociaria, its art, history,
culture. COURSES seminars FELLOWSHIPS nil PUBLICATIONS "Bollet-
tino" (variable dates of issue, 1977–87); *Annali del centro di studi soriani*
(1988-) annual; "Umanisti di Ciociaria" [i.e. Southern Latium] (series); "Fonti
e Studi Baroniani" (series)

57. **Centro di Studi sulla Civiltà del Tardo Medioevo**
Loggiati di S. Domenico, San Miniato (Pisa), Italy
TEL (0571) 40.01.51 / 41.82.51 OFFICERS Dir. Sergio Gensini Pres. Paolo
Brezzi FOUNDED 1985 AFFILIATION ind. LIBRARY nil ACTIVITIES col-
loquia, seminars COURSES nil FELLOWSHIPS available for the seminars
PUBLICATIONS conference proceedings

58. **Centro di Studi sulla Cultura e l'Immagine di Roma**
c/o Accademia Nazionale dei Lincei, Via della Lungara 10, 00165 Roma, Italy
TEL (06) 65.08.31 OFFICERS Pres. Francesco Gabrieli; Vice-Pres. Cesare
Brandi; Dir. Marcello Fagiolo FOUNDED 1980 AFFILIATION Ministero per
i Beni Culturali e Ambientali; Accademia Nazionale dei Lincei; Istituto della

Enciclopedia Italiana RESEARCH INTERESTS Rome, especially during the Renaissance and the Baroque eras ACTIVITIES seminars, conferences, exhibitions, publication of conference proceedings PUBLICATIONS conference proceedings (13 vols. to date)

59. **Centro di Studi sull'Umanesimo Meridionale**
Università di Salerno, I-84000 Fisciano (SA), Italy
TEL (089) 96.24.26 OFFICERS Dir. Prof. Gioacchino Paparelli FOUNDED 1975 AFFILIATION ind. LIBRARY nil (uses the university library) RESEARCH INTERESTS history, literature, philology of the 15th and 16th centuries ACTIVITIES trimonthly seminars COURSES only those given by the university FELLOWSHIPS nil PUBLICATIONS *Misure critiche* (journal)

60. **Centro di Studi sul Teatro Medioevale e Rinascimentale (Viterbo)**
has now moved to Rome under the name Centro Studi sul Teatro Medioevale e Rinascimentale (q.v.)

61. **Centro di Studi su Matteo Bandello e la Cultura Rinascimentale**
c/o Biblioteca Civica, piazza A. Arzano 2, 15057 Tortona (Alessandria), Italy
TEL (0131) 86.42.73 OFFICERS Pres. Mario Pozzi; Secr. Ugo Rozzo FOUNDED 1980 AFFILIATION ind. LIBRARY nil ACTIVITIES research on and edition of the works of Matteo Bandello and northern Italian Renaissance "novellistica" PUBLICATIONS Bollettino del Centro; texts; conference proceedings (1982, 1984)

62. **Centro di Studi Tassiani**
Piazza Vecchia 15, I-24100 Bergamo, Italy
TEL 39–9430 OFFICERS Pres. Aldo Agazzi; Secr. Prof. Marcello Ballini; Dir. Gianni Barachetti FOUNDED 1950 MEMBERSHIP n/a LIBRARY affiliation with the Biblioteca Civica SPECIALIZATION HOURS 8h30–12h30; 14h30–18h30; closed Wednesday afternoons, and holidays ANNUAL CLOSURE 15–20 August RESEARCH INTERESTS Bernardo Tasso, Torquato Tasso ACTIVITIES conferences, seminars, etc. on the two Tassos COURSES nil FELLOWSHIPS nil PUBLICATIONS *Studi Tassiani*, vol. 1 (1951) (annual); vol. 35 (1987)

63. **Centro di Studi Umanistici**
Istituto di Filologia Moderna, Facoltà di Lettere, I-98100 Messina, Italy
TEL (090) 77–2005 OFFICERS Pres. Prof. Gianvito Resta (1988–90) FOUNDED 1981 par les membres de l'Istituto di Filologia Moderna MEMBERSHIP gratuit AFFILIATION Istituto di Filologia Moderna LIBRARY nil RESEARCH INTERESTS philologie et litérature; histoire de la culture de la Renaissance ACTIVITIES colloques, séminaires, conférences COURSES nil FELLOWSHIPS nil PUBLICATIONS *Rivista di Filologia Umanistica* (annuel); "Studi e Testi" (series, 8 vols. jusqu'au présent)

64. **Centro Europeo di Ricerche sul Viaggio in Italia (CERVI)**
Strada Revigliasco 6, I-10024 Moncallieri (Torino), Italy
TEL 640–7488. No further information available at this time

65. **Centro Interdipartimentale di Studi Rinascimentali**
Università di Roma II, Tor Vergata (Roma), Italy
No further information available at this time

66. **Centro Internazionale di Studi di Architettura "Andrea Palladio"**
Domus Comestabilis, Basilica Palladiana, Palazzo Valmarana Braga, I-36100
Vicenza, Italy
TEL (0444) 54.61.88 OFFICERS Pres. Antonio Corazzini; Secr. Renato Cevese
FOUNDED 1958 LIBRARY "Raccolta palladiana Cappelletti" (ca. 600 vols.
and articles); fototeca (18,000 photographs and 5,000 slides) RESEARCH
INTERESTS Palladio and Italian architecture in the Renaissance ACTIVI-
TIES seminars, conferences, etc. COURSES "Corsi Internazionali di Storia
dell'Architettura" FELLOWSHIPS nil PUBLICATIONS "Bollettino", vol. 1
(1959) (newsletter) "Corpus Palladianum" (series)

67. **Centro Internazionale di Studi Umanistici**
c/o Facoltà di Filosofia, Università degli Studi, Via Nomentana 118, I-00161
Roma, Italy
TEL n/a OFFICERS Pres. Prof. Ernesto Grassi; Vice-Pres. Prof. Sergio Cotta;
Secr. Paolo Castelli Gattinara FOUNDED 1978 MEMBERSHIP n/a AFFILIA-
TION Istituto di Studi Filosofici LIBRARY access to university library RE-
SEARCH INTERESTS Italian humanism ACTIVITIES annual conferences
(January); occasional conferences. COURSES n/a FELLOWSHIPS n/a PUBLI-
CATIONS *Archivio di Filosofia*, vol. 1; "Classici del Pensiero Italiano" (series;
already published the *Opera omnia* of Pico della Mirandola, Coluccio Salutati,
Giacomo Acconcio, Egidio da Viterbo, Pietro Crinito, Tommaso Campanella);
Testi Umanistici sull'Ermetismo; *Testi Umanistici sulla Retorica*

68. **Centro per il Collegamento degli Studi Medioevali e Umanistici**
c/o Istituto di Filologia Latina, Facoltà di magistero, Università degli Studi, Via
del Tartaro 61, I-06100 Perugia, Italy
TEL 2–6050 OFFICERS Dir. Prof. Claudio Leonardi FOUNDED n/a MEM-
BERSHIP n/a AFFILIATION Università degli Studi, Perugia LIBRARY access to university library RESEARCH INTERESTS n/a ACTIVITIES n/a
COURSES n/a FELLOWSHIPS n/a PUBLICATIONS n/a

69. **Centro per la Storia della Tradizione Aristotelica**
Università di Padova, Padova, Italy
No further information available at this time

70. **Centro per Ricerche di Filosofia Medievale**
c/o Facoltà di Magistero, Istituto di Storia della Filosofia, Università degli Studi,

Piazza Capitanato 3, I-35100 Padova, Italy
TEL (049) 66–2550 OFFICERS Dir. Prof. Antonio Tognolo FOUNDED 1965 MEMBERSHIP n/a AFFILIATION Università degli Studi, Padova LIBRARY access to university library RESEARCH INTERESTS research in philosophic thought from the Middle Ages to Humanism and the Renaissance. PUBLICA-TIONS *Medioevo*, vol. 1 (1975) (annual)

71. **Centro Studi del Pensiero Filosofico del '500 e '600**
via Albricci 9, I-20122 Milano, Italy
TEL 805.2538 OFFICERS Arrigo Pacchi AFFILIATION C.N.R., Università di Milano LIBRARY 1000 vols. RESEARCH INTERESTS philosophie, religion, pensée politique des 16 et 17 siècles ACTIVITIES un colloque tous les deux ans COURSES nil FELLOWSHIPS nil

72. **Centro Studi "Europa delle Corti"**
c/o Prof. Mozzarelli, Università di Trento, Trento, Italy
TEL n/a OFFICERS Pres. Prof. Amedeo Quondam; Secr. Prof. Cesare Mozzarelli FOUNDED 1976 MEMBERSHIP n/a AFFILIATION Ind. LIBRARY n/a RESEARCH INTERESTS cultural, social, institutional, and art history of Ancien Regime; courts ACTIVITIES annual colloquium PUBLICATIONS *Biblioteca del Cinquecento*

73. **Centro Studi Rinascimento Musicale**
Villa Medicea "La Ferdinanda", Via Papa Giovanni XXIII, I-50040 Artimino (Firenze), Italy
TEL (055) 871–8082 OFFICERS Pres. and Artistic Dir. Annibale Gianuarlo FOUNDED 1969 MEMBERSHIP n/a AFFILIATION n/a LIBRARY n/a RE-SEARCH INTERESTS Italian Renaissance music ACTIVITIES see above under Publications. COURSES n/a FELLOWSHIPS n/a PUBLICATIONS works by Claudio Monteverdi, Giulio Caccini, Jacopo Peri, Domenico Mazzocchi; reprints of original editions; reviews of Renaissance music

74. **Centro Studi sul Teatro Medioevale e Rinascimentale**
Casa del Teatro E.T.I., Via in Arcione 98, I-00187 Roma, Italy
TEL (06) 67.20.21 (mornings) and 46.28.23 OFFICERS Dir. Federico Doglio FOUNDED 1975 (in Viterbo; transferred to Rome in 1986) RESEARCH IN-TERESTS medieval and Renaissance theatre PUBLICATIONS conference proceedings (12 volumes to date); catalogue, published through Coletti Editore, via Clitunno 24F, Roma

75. **Centrum Renaissancedrama**
Prinsstraat 13, B-2000 Antwerpen, Belgium
TEL 32–3–220–42–88 OFFICERS Dir. Dr G. Van Eemeren (1984–   ); Dr. H. Meeus FOUNDED 1972, by Prof. Dr. L. Rens (Director 1972–1983) MEM-BERSHIP n/a AFFILIATION Universitaire Faculteiten St-Ignatius, Antwerp (UFSIA) LIBRARY 120 rare books; 1500 modern imprints; 250 microforms; 5

journals; SPECIALIZATION Western European 16th-17th cent. drama, esp.
of the Netherlands HOURS 9–12h, 13–16h ANNUAL CLOSURE nil RE-
SEARCH INTERESTS history of Dutch Renaissance drama ACTIVITIES occasional colloquia and seminars COURSES nil FELLOWSHIPS assistance of
outside researchers at our centre PUBLICATIONS several books and articles
on Renaissance drama in the Netherlands

76. **Columbia University Seminar on the Renaissance**
c/o Renaissance Society of America, 1161 Amsterdam Avenue, New York, NY
10027, USA
TEL (212) 280–2318 OFFICERS Chair Richard Harris; Secr. Peter Ruduytchy
FOUNDED n/a MEMBERSHIP n/a AFFILIATION Columbia University LI-
BRARY nil RESEARCH INTERESTS all fields in the Renaissance ACTIVI-
TIES seminars COURSES nil FELLOWSHIPS nil PUBLICATIONS nil

77. **Commission for Renaissance Studies**
s. dm. Ulianova 19, Moscow 117036, USSR
TEL 1239013 OFFICERS V.N. Grascenkov FOUNDED 1972 MEMBERSHIP
gratuit AFFILIATION USSR Academy of Science LIBRARY nil RESEARCH
INTERESTS the Renaissance in Europe ACTIVITIES annual colloquia; conferences every three years COURSES nil FELLOWSHIPS nil PUBLICATIONS
conference proceedings

78. **Commission pour l'Etude de la Renaissance et Reformation**
c/o Prof. Lech Szczucki, Instytut Filozofii i Socjologii PAN, PL-00330
Warszawa, Poland
TEL 26–52–31 ext. 35 OFFICERS Prof. Lech Szczucki (Pres. 1984–1988)
FOUNDED 1970 MEMBERSHIP 70 members; no fees AFFILIATION Pol-
ish Academy of Sciences LIBRARY nil RESEARCH INTERESTS interdisciplinary research on the Renaissance and Reformation ACTIVITIES annual or
semi-annual conferences COURSES nil FELLOWSHIPS nil PUBLICATIONS
Newsletter (non-periodical)

79. **Committee for Medieval Studies**
c/o Dean of Arts, University of British Columbia, 1866 Main Mall, Vancouver,
B.C., Canada V6T 1W5
TEL (604) 228–5165 OFFICERS Chair Prof. A. Jean Elder (1988–89)
FOUNDED 1970 MEMBERSHIP 30 AFFILIATION Univ. of British Columbia
LIBRARY nil RESEARCH INTERESTS The Committee has more than 30
members whose research interests range widely across history, art and literature of Medieval and Renaissance Europe, from 10th-century Byzantine church
music to 16th-century French urban politics. ACTIVITIES Annual Workshop
(conference) in the second week of November, each year on a selected topic.
COURSES yes, towards a B.A. FELLOWSHIPS nil PUBLICATIONS *Studies
in Medieval and Renaissance History* (annual) (1978-)

80. **Courtauld Institute of Art**
    20 Portman Square, London W1H 0BE, England
    TEL (01) 935–9292–5 or 486–5913–4 OFFICERS Chairman Sir Nicholas
    Goodison; Dir Prof. C.M. Kauffmann FOUNDED 1932 MEMBERSHIP n/a
    AFFILIATION London University LIBRARY 100,000 vols (50,000 books, rare
    and modern imprints; 50,000 pamphlets; microforms; 187 journals) PHOTO-
    GRAPHIC LIBRARY Witt Library European paintings from 1200 to present
    (1.5 m. photographs); Conway Library medieval art, European architecture
    and sculpture (1 m. photographs) SPECIALIZATION history of European
    art HOURS 9h30–19h00 during term; 2h30–18h00 during vacations; visitors
    should apply to the librarian on duty for admission ANNUAL CLOSURE part
    of August RESEARCH INTERESTS history of European art, early Christian
    to 20th century; science of the conservation of paintings ACTIVITIES two an-
    nual lecture series (public). There are 7 teachers covering painting, sculpture
    and architecture in the period 1350–1650 COURSES yes, towards a B.A., an
    M.A., a Ph.D., a Post Graduate Diploma (1 year), a Diploma in Conservation of
    Paintings and Wall Paintings (3 years) FELLOWSHIPS nil GALLERIES PUB-
    LICATIONS *Journal of the Warburg and Courtauld Institutes*, vol. 1 (annual);
    Prospectus, vol. 1 (annual)

81. **Cusanus Commission der Heidelberger Akademie**
    Karlsplatz 4, D-6900 Heidelberg, West Germany
    OFFICERS Dr. Werner Bererwaltes. No further information available at this
    time

82. **Dansk Selskab for Oldtids og Middelalderforskning (Danish Society for
    Research of Ancient and Medieval Times)**
    Nationalmuseet, Frederiksholms kanal 12, DK-1200 Købehavn K, Denmark
    TEL (01) 13.44.11 OFFICERS Pres. (1987–90) Søren Dietz Secr. (1987–90)
    Jørgen Steen Jensen FOUNDED 1984 MEMBERSHIP 120 AFFILIATION
    Danish National Museum LIBRARY nil RESEARCH INTERESTS Ancient
    and Medieval History ACTIVITIES ca. 5 meetings a year, for elected members
    only COURSES nil FELLOWSHIPS nil PUBLICATIONS *Classica et Mediae-
    valia* (34 vols. to date)

83. **Deutsche Shakespeare-Gesellschaft West**
    Rathaus, D-4360 Bochum, West Germany
    TEL (0234) 31–1842 OFFICERS Pres. Prof. Werner Habicht; Chair Prof.
    Dr. Borgmeier FOUNDED 1963 MEMBERSHIP 1755 AFFILIATION ind.
    LIBRARY affiliated with the Shakespeare Bibliothek, Universität München,
    Schellingstr. 3, 8000 München 40, West Germany SPECIALIZATION HOURS
    consult with the Shakespeare Bibliothek (above) RESEARCH INTERESTS
    Shakespeare and Elizabethan Drama ACTIVITIES nil COURSES nil FEL-
    LOWSHIPS nil PUBLICATIONS *Deutsche Shakespeare-Gesellschaft (West)
    Jahrbuch*, vol. 1

84. **Dolmetsch Foundation**
High Pines, Wood Road, Hindhead, Surrey, England
TEL n/a OFFICERS Pres. The Hon. Mrs. Maurice Macmillan; Chair John C. Slugden; Secr. Mrs P. Dutton FOUNDED 1928 MEMBERSHIP 900 AFFIL-IATION n/a LIBRARY n/a RESEARCH INTERESTS in international society for early music and instruments ACTIVITIES sponsors the annual Haslemere Festival COURSES n/a FELLOWSHIPS n/a PUBLICATIONS *The Consort*, vol. 1 (annual); "The Bulletin" (2 p.a.)

85. **Early English Text Society**
c/o T.F. Hoad, Executive Secretary, Early English Text Society, St Peter's College, Oxford, OX1 2DL, England
TEL n/a OFFICERS Dir. Prof. John Burrow (Dept of English, Bristol Univ.); Editorial Secr. Dr. Malcolm Godden (Exeter College, Oxford OX1 3DP); Executive Secr. Mr. T.F. Hoad (St Peter's College, Oxford OX1 2DL); Assist. Exec. Secr. Mrs. Wendy Collier (The Vicarage, Hope, Sheffield S30 2RN) FOUNDED 1864, by Frederick James Furnivall, with help of Richard Morris, Walter Skeat, and others MEMBERSHIP ca. 1050 (ca. 630 individuals, 420 institutions; £15, US$30, CAN$35) AFFILIATION ind. LIBRARY nil RESEARCH INTERESTS n/a ACTIVITIES the publication of English texts earlier than 1558 COURSES nil FELLOWSHIPS nil PUBLICATIONS English texts earlier than 1558 (one or more vols p.a.)

86. **Early Music Institute**
Indiana University, Bloomington, IN 47401, USA
TEL (812) 335–4088 OFFICERS Dir. Prof. Thomas Binkley FOUNDED 1980 MEMBERSHIP n/a AFFILIATION Indiana University, School of Music LIBRARY nil RESEARCH INTERESTS performance practices from the Medieval to the Baroque ACTIVITIES seminars, conferences, performances; publication of editions, studies, and records COURSES yes, towards a B.M., M.M., D.M., Ph.D. FELLOWSHIPS yes, inquire with the Institute PUBLICATIONS "Music Scholarship and Performance" (series, publ. by Indiana UP; book-length contributions to historical performance of any period); "Early Music Studies" (series of publications, small to medium length); "Focus Records" (6 p.a.)

87. **Ente Casa Buonarroti**
Via Ghibellina 70, I-50122 Firenze, Italy
TEL (055) 24–1752 OFFICERS Pres. Prof. Paola Barocchi; Dir. Dr. Pina Ragionieri; Secr.-Treas. Sign. Pasquale Sassu FOUNDED 1858, by will of Cosimo Buonarroti MEMBERSHIP n/a AFFILIATION Ministero per i Beni Culturali e Ambientali LIBRARY ca 4000 vols.; mss, rare books, modern imprints, journals SPECIALIZATION Archivio Buonarroti; Fondo Charles De Tolnay; Fondo Jacques Mesnil HOURS 9–13h, weekdays; letter of introduction from the visitor's institution is required ANNUAL CLOSURE n/a RESEARCH

INTERESTS history of the Buonarroti family, which lived in the palazzo in Via Ghibellina ACTIVITIES occasional conferences, seminars, colloquia, exhibitions. COURSES n/a FELLOWSHIPS n/a PUBLICATIONS exhibition catalogues

88. **Erasmus Commissie (Commission Erasme)**
Herengracht 410–412, 1017 BX Amsterdam, Pays-Bas
TEL (020) 23–8439 OFFICERS Dir Dr. J. Trapman FOUNDED n/a MEMBERSHIP n/a AFFILIATION Académie Royale Néerlandaise des Sciences et des Sciences Humaines LIBRARY seule bibl. d'usuels; ca. 1000 vois. SPECIALIZATION Erasme HOURS pas d'entrée pour le public ANNUAL CLOSURE RESEARCH INTERESTS Erasme ACTIVITIES publication de l'*Opera Omnia* d'Erasme COURSES nil FELLOWSHIPS nil PUBLICATIONS *Opera Omnia Erasmi Roterodami*

89. **Erasmus of Rotterdam Society**
2217 Old Fort Hills Drive, Fort Washington, MD 20744, USA
TEL (301) 292–7598 OFFICERS have no fixed terms: Pres. Prof. J.-C. Margolin (France) (1988–); Vice-Pres. Prof. Clarence H. Miller (USA) (1980–); Secr.-Treasurer Dr. Richard L. DeMolen (USA) (1980–); Past Presidents Prof. Roland H. Bainton (1980–84); Dr. Margaret Mann Phillips (1984–88) FOUNDED 1980 by R.L. DeMolenMEMBERSHIP 600 individual ($30) and institutional ($35) AFFILIATION ind. LIBRARY 500 books (60 rare books, 20 engravings, 440 modern imprints, 6 journals) SPECIALIZATION Erasmus of Rotterdam and his critics HOURS by appointment only ANNUAL CLOSURE national and religious holidays RESEARCH INTERESTS Erasmus of Rotterdam and his critics ACTIVITIES Birthday Lecture (27 October) at the Folger Library; Bainton Lecture (25 April) at the Warburg Institute; Phillips Lecture (12 July) at the Royal Netherlands Embassy (Washington, D.C., USA). COURSES nil FELLOWSHIPS nil PUBLICATIONS *Erasmus of Rotterdam Society Yearbook*, vol. 1 (1981); Proceedings from selected annual conferences; etc.

90. **Europa delle Corti. Centro studi sulle società di antico regime**
Dipartimento di discipline storiche, Università di Bologna, Bologna, Italy
TEL n/a OFFICERS Pres. Prof. Amedeo Quondam; Secr. Prof. Cesare Mozzarelli FOUNDED 1976 MEMBERSHIP Lire 20,000 AFFILIATION ind. LIBRARY nil RESEARCH INTERESTS Ancien Regime ACTIVITIES annual seminar COURSES nil FELLOWSHIPS nil PUBLICATIONS collection of works (42 to date) published by Bulzoni Editore, Rome, Italy

91. **Fédération Internationale des Sociétés et Instituts pour l'Etude de la Renaissance (FISIER)**
rue du Péri 41, B-4000 Liège, Belgium
OFFICERS Pres. Prof. Léon-E. Halkin; Sec. (USA) Prof. Robert M. Kingdon

(Inst. for Research in the Humanities, Univ. of Wisconsin, Madison, Wisc. 53706, USA). No further information available at this time

92. **Federazione Nazionale di Istituti e Centri in Italia**
c/o Istituto di Studi Rinascimentali, Palazzo Paradiso, Via Scienze 17, I-44100 Ferrara, Italy
TEL (0532) 76.00.02 and 33.227 OFFICERS Pres. Prof. Gianvito Renza; Dir. Prof. Gianni Venturi FOUNDED 1989 ACTIVITIES to promote communication and collaboration among Italian institutes and centres devoted to the Renaissance

93. **Folger Institute**
Folger Shakespeare Library, 201 East Capitol Street S.E., Washington, DC 20003, USA
TEL (202) 544–4600 OFFICERS Chair Barbara A. Mowat; Exec. Dir. Lena Cowen Orlin FOUNDED 1970 MEMBERSHIP 23 co-operating universities AFFILIATION The Folger Shakespeare Library LIBRARY Folger Shakespeare Library SPECIALIZATION Renaissance, Shakespeare, and 18th Century Studies HOURS 8h45–16h45 Monday to Saturday; access with postdoctoral references ANNUAL CLOSURE nil RESEARCH INTERESTS Early modern studies ACTIVITIES conferences, seminars, colloquia COURSES yes; contact the Institute FELLOWSHIPS yes; contact the Institute EXTRACT FROM BROCHURE A collaborative enterprise co-sponsored by 23 major universities, the Institute offers a complex interdisciplinary program of seminars, workshops, symposia, colloquia, and lectures. The library holds the largest collection of English Renaissance books outside the British Isles, as well as extensive collections in the English 17th and 18th centuries, in the Continental Renaissance, and in English and American theatre history from their beginnings to the 20th century PUBLICATIONS *Shakespeare Quarterly*, vol. 1; Proceedings of conferences

94. **Fondazione Giorgio Cini**
Isola S. Giorgio Maggiore, I-30124 Venezia, Italy
TEL (41 Venezia) 528–9900; Telex 431484 CINEND; Telefax 041/5238540 OFFICERS Pres. Bruno Visentini; Secr. General Vittore Branca FOUNDED 1951 by Count Vittorio Cini MEMBERSHIP n/a AFFILIATION ind. LIBRARY yes; ca. 90,000 vols., 1000 rare books; drawings SPECIALIZATION history of Venetian civilization and problems of modern society HOURS 9h30–12h30, 14h30–16h30 ANNUAL CLOSURE some days in middle August RESEARCH INTERESTS see above ACTIVITIES conferences, colloquia, seminars, research and courses, exhibitions, concerts COURSES yes; graduate and post-graduate specialisation FELLOWSHIPS nil PUBLICATIONS "Notiziario di San Giorgio", (irregular) (Newsletter); proceedings; etc. and more than 200 titles of various publishers

95. **Fondazione Giovanni Pierluigi da Palestrina**
    Centro di Studi Palestriniani, Vicolo del Giardino 15, I-00036 Palestrina (Roma), Italy
    TEL (06) 358–7212 or 955–8083 OFFICERS Dir. Lino Bianchi; Dir. Artistico Giancarlo Rostirolla; Secr. Gen. Luigi Puliti FOUNDED n/a MEMBERSHIP n/a AFFILIATION ind. LIBRARY modern imprints and journals SPECIAL-IZATION Renaissance and Palestrinian tradition HOURS by appointment only ANNUAL CLOSURE nil RESEARCH INTERESTS Italy and Europe; Palestrina and his contemporaries; the Palestrinian tradition in the world ACTIVITIES colloquia COURSES nil FELLOWSHIPS nil PUBLICATIONS proceedings from conferences on Palestrina; facsimile reprints of sources for Palestrina

96. **Forum for Renæssancestudier**
    c/o Institut for Klassisk Filologi, Københavns Universitet, Njalsgade 94, DK-2300 København S, Denmark
    TEL 1 (45) 1–54–22–11 OFFICERS Marianne Alenius, Karsten Friis-Jensen, Eric Jacobsen, Hannemarie Ragn Jensen, Minna Skafte Jensen, Peter Ulf Møller, Marianne Pade, Lene Waage Petersen, Peter Zeeberg, Knud Prange FOUNDED 1984 MEMBERSHIP informal association of students and teachers AFFILIATION Dept of Classics, Univ. of Copenhagen LIBRARY n/a RESEARCH INTERESTS neo-latin literature; Danish learned women; Italian humanist translation of Greek classics; Italian vernacular Renaissance literature; Italian Renaissance art ACTIVITIES informal meetings, seminars, lectures; publications of materials such as newsletters, anthologies, monographs, and editions are planned for the future PUBLICATIONS "Renæssancestudier" (Renaissance Studies) [distributor Museum Tusculanum Press, Njalsgade 94, DK-2300, København S, Denmark); the "Forum" runs the Danish branch of the Inter-Nordic research project *Nordic Literature in Latin and its Connections with Europe*

97. **Francis Bacon Foundation**
    655 North Dartmouth Ave., Claremont, CA 91711, USA
    TEL (714) 624–6305 OFFICERS Pres. Elizabeth S. Wrigley (1988–89); Secr.-Treasurer Emrys J. Ross (1988–89); Librarian Jacqueline Bellows (1986–) FOUNDED 1938 by Louise Stevens and Walter Conrad Arensberg MEMBER-SHIP n/a AFFILIATION Claremont Graduate School LIBRARY 13,000 vols (40 mss, 2887 pre-1800 imprints; 10,000 modern imprints, 79 microforms, 49 journals) SPECIALIZATION Francis Bacon, his life, works, and influence on his own and succeeding times; Tudor and Stuart literature and history, history of science; Shakespeare authorship controversy; cryptography; Rosicrucianism; alchemy; witchcraft and magic. HOURS 9h00–16h30 Monday to Friday; open to the public; reader's card necessary to consult rare books ANNUAL CLOSURE nil RESEARCH INTERESTS Francis Bacon; Elizabethan and Jacobean literature, history, science, and culture. ACTIVITIES Annual Bacon

lecture (Jan.), as well as other lectures, and exhibitions; assists in supporting the Annual Renaissance Conference of Southern California COURSES nil FEL-LOWSHIPS nil PUBLICATIONS Long and short-title catalogues of various of the Library's collections.

98. **Francis Bacon Society, Inc.**
   Reg. Office, Canonbury Tower, Islington, London N1, England
   TEL n/a OFFICERS Pres. J.D. Maconachie; Chair Noel Fermor FOUNDED 1886 MEMBERSHIP n/a AFFILIATION n/a LIBRARY n/a RESEARCH IN-TERESTS to study the works and the life of Francis Bacon and evidence in respect to the authorship of the plays attributed to Shakespeare. ACTIVITIES n/a COURSES n/a FELLOWSHIPS n/a PUBLICATIONS *Baconiana*, vol. 1; *Jottings*, vol. 1 (annual)

99. **Hakluyt Society**
   c/o Map Library, The British Library, Great Russell Street, London WC1B 3DG, England
   TEL (025) 125–4207 OFFICERS Pres. Sir Harold Smedley, K.C.M.G., M.B.E.; Hon. Secretaries Dr T.E. Armstrong, Mrs Sarah Tyacke FOUNDED 1846 MEMBERSHIP 2,300 AFFILIATION ind. LIBRARY nil RESEARCH INTER-ESTS historical travel (geography) ACTIVITIES publication of the Hakluyt Society texts COURSES nil FELLOWSHIPS nil EXTRACT FROM BROCHURE The Hakluyt Society has for its object the advancement of education by the publication of scholarly editions of records of voyages, travels, and other ge-ographical material of the past. The Society has not confined its selection to the works of English travellers, to a particular age, or to particular regions. Where the original is foreign, the work is given in English, either a fresh trans-lation being made, or an earlier rendering, accurate as well as attractive, being utilised. One hundred volumes (forming Series I) were issued from 1847 to 1898; 169 vols. of Series II have been issued in the years 1898–1985; and 42 in an Extra Series to date (1986). Annual subscription (in 1986) £15 or US$30, payable on 1st January each year; cheques payable to The Hakluyt Society PUBLICATIONS Hakluyt Society Second Series and Extra Series

100. **Institut de Recherches et d'Histoire des Textes**
    40 avenue d'Iéna, F-75116 Paris, France
    TEL 47–23–6104 OFFICERS Dir. Prof. Louis Holtz (1986–   ); Section d'humanisme Edith Bayle FOUNDED 1937 par Félix Grat MEMBERSHIP n/a AFFILIATION Centre National de la Recherche Scientifique LIBRARY 80,000 vols.; 450 revues SPECIALIZATION Manuscrit médiéval; Textes de l'Antiquité et du Moyen-Age; Humanisme; sources documentaires sur l'histoire de France HOURS 9h00–18h00 RESEARCH INTERESTS Manuscrit médiéval et livre ancien; litterature de l'Antiquité et du Moyen Age ACTIVITIES Recherche et documentation, microfilm; colloques COURSES nil FELLOW-SHIPS nil PUBLICATIONS *Revue d'Histoire des Textes*, vol. 1 (1971) (an-

nuelle); *Bibliographie internationale de l'Humanisme et de la Renaissance*, vol. 1 (1964) (annuelle); "Nouvelles du livre ancien", vol. 1 (1974) (trimestriel); "Nouvelles des empreints/Fingerprint newsletter", vol. 1 (1981); 2 (1985)

101. **Institut d'Etudes de la Renaissance et de l'Age Classique**
Maison Rhône-Alpes des Sciences de l'Homme, Université de Saint-Etienne, 35 rue du Onze Novembre, F-42023 Saint-Etienne Cedex 2, France TEL 77–42–16–71 OFFICERS Prof. Claude Longeon FOUNDED 1980 (fait suite au Centre de la Renaissance et de l'Age Baroque fondé en 1974) MEMBERSHIP n/a AFFILIATION Univ. de Saint-Etienne LIBRARY 2,000 imprimés moderns; 150 microfilms; 25 périodiques. HOURS 9h00–16h00, du lundi au vendredi; ouverte aux chercheurs et étudiants ANNUAL CLOSURE août RESEARCH INTERESTS civilisation de la Renaissance européenne, XVe au XVIIe siècle; en particuliers, humanisme, théâtre, littérature romanesque et polémique ACTIVITIES colloques, occasionnellement. COURSES tronc commun & spécialités dans littérature française. Diplôme d'Etudes Approfondies, Diplôme Universitaire d'Etudes et de Recherches, Doctorat FELLOWSHIPS nil PUBLICATIONS "Répertoire International des Seiziémistes"; travaux, textes, éditions critiques

102. **Institut d'Etudes Médiévales**
Collège Erasme, Place Blaise Pascal 1, B-1348 Louvain-la-Neuve, Belgium TEL (010) 43.48.65 / 43.48.61 OFFICERS Pres. Mme J. Hamesse; Secr. Jean-Marie Yante FOUNDED n/a MEMBERSHIP n/a AFFILIATION Univ. Catholique de Louvain LIBRARY universitaire HOURS 8h30–21h00, lundi-samedi, avec une Carte d'accès ANNUAL CLOSURE n/a RESEARCH INTERESTS l'institut a pour but de promouvoir les recherches interdisciplinaires et la formation de médiévalistes largement informés des multiples aspects de la civilisation médiévale, de manière à favoriser la compréhension plénière des phénomènes historiques dans toute leur complexité ACTIVITIES Congrès 1975 "Les universités à la fin du Moyen Age"; Congrès 1981 "Les genres littéraires dans les sources théologiques et philosophiques"; Congrès 1987 "Le travail du Moyen Age. Une approche interdisciplinaire" COURSES "Diplôme d'Etudes Médiévales" et "Doctorat en Histoire de la Civilisation Médiévale" FELLOWSHIPS convention d'échange de bourses pour post-gradués avec l'Università Cattolica del Sacro Cuore de Milan; échange de professeurs avec la même université ainsi qu'avec l'Univ. Catholique de Louvain PUBLICATIONS *Typologie des Sources du Moyen Age Occidental* (48 fasc. parus); *Textes, Etudes, Congrès* (6 vols. parus)

103. **Institut d'Histoire de la Réformation**
c/o Bibliothèque publique et universitaire, CH-1211 Genève 4, Suisse TEL (0041–22) 20–93–33 int. 2128 OFFICERS Dir. Prof. Francis Higman FOUNDED 1969 MEMBERSHIP n/a AFFILIATION Univ. de Genève LIBRARY 9500 vols.; Collection Trouchin (135 vols., corresp. 16e-17e siècles);

ca. 2500 livres anciens; ca. 6500 imprimés modernes; 400 microfilms. Accès à la collection de la Bibl. publ. et univ. (1,000,000 vols.) et a celle du Musée historique de la Réformation. SPECIALIZATION Calviniana; histoire de l'exégèse biblique HOURS 8–12h, 14h00–18h00, lundi-vendredi ANNUAL CLOSURE permanence non assurée en juillet-août RESEARCH INTERESTS controverses religieuses du 16e siècle; histoire de l'exégèse biblique; Jean Calvin; Martin Bucer; Théodore de Bèze; traductions latines des Pères grecs; dissidence religieuse; John Locke exégète biblique; inventaire de la correspondance et étude de la théologie de Jean-Alphonse Turrettini; travaux bibliographiques sur la Réforme ACTIVITIES colloques mensuels; congrès occasionnels COURSES direction de thèses de doctorat et de diplômes FELLOWSHIPS bourses de 3 mois (ca. FS 1000/mois) pour des étudiants étrangers; possibilités d'obtenir une bourse de la Confédération EXTRACT FROM BROCHURE L'Institut constitue un des 'centres' de l'Université de Genève. Il a pour but de préparer les éditions critiques des oeuvres théologiques des 16e-18e siècles et de diriger les travaux des étudiants avancés qui préparent un doctorat ou un diplôme d'études avancées soit à l'Univ. de Genève soit ailleurs. L'enseignement se fait en langue française, anglaise et allemande. L'Institut accueille également des enseignants universitaires étrangers en congé sabbatique. PUBLICATIONS L'Institut participe à la publication de *Corpus Catholicorum*, *Martini Buceri Opera Latina*, *Erasmi Opera Omnia*, *Bibliotheca dissentium*, *Catalogus Translationum*

104. **Institut d'Histoire de le Renaissance et de la Réforme**
Faculté de philosophie et lettres, 3 Place Cockerill, B-4000 Liège, Belgium TEL (41) 42–0080 ext.   461 OFFICERS Dir. Prof. Jean-Pierre Massaut FOUNDED n/a MEMBERSHIP n/a AFFILIATION Univ. de Liège LIBRARY 10,000 vols; 100 livres rares; 50 microfilms SPECIALIZATION Fond des martyrologes protestants HOURS 9–12h, 14–17h, lundi-vendredi ANNUAL CLOSURE 20 juillet 20 août RESEARCH INTERESTS histoire religieuse; Erasmus; humanisme chrétien; Luther; théologie et spiritualité des XVe, XVIe, XVIIe siècles; histoire de l'éducation et de la pédagogie; manuels scolaires; écoles latines ACTIVITIES colloques occasionnels; séminaires hebdomodaires COURSES histoire de la Renaissance; histoire de la Réforme; histoire du livre; Latin de la Renaissance; Séminaire. Certificat d'études complémentaires en histoire de la Renaissance et de la Réforme FELLOWSHIPS nil PUBLICATIONS travaux dans "Bibliothèque de la Faculté de Philosophie et Lettres de l'Université de Liège"

105. **Institut d'études médiévales**
C.P. 6128, Succ. "A", Montréal, Québec, Canada H3C 3J7 TEL (514) 343–7609 ou 343–6486 OFFICERS Dir. Prof. Claude Sutto FOUNDED n/a MEMBERSHIP n/a AFFILIATION Université de Montréal LIBRARY ca. 100,000 vols 3 mss; 1000 livres anciens; 99,000 imprimés

modernes; 1000 microfilms; 150 périodiques HOURS 9h00–17h00 lundi au vendredi ANNUAL CLOSURE en général, les deux dernières semaines de juillet RESEARCH INTERESTS patristique; histoire de France, XIVe et XVe siècles; histoire de l'Eglise, Ve au XVe siècle; sciences auxiliaires; littérature française, XIIe au XVe siècle; philosophie. ACTIVITIES colloque annuel (fin avril ou début mai) COURSES Maîtrise et Doctorat FELLOWSHIPS nil PUBLICATIONS travaux, séries, textes et éditions critiques, traductions

106. **Institute for Early Contact Period Studies**
2121 GPA, University of Florida, Gainesville, FL 32611, USA
TEL (305) 392–1503 OFFICERS Dir. Prof. Michael V. Gannon FOUNDED 1985, in anticipation of the 500th anniv. of Columbus' voyage MEMBERSHIP n/a AFFILIATION n/a LIBRARY n/a RESEARCH INTERESTS travel and relations between Europeans and American Indians, 1492–1542 ACTIVITIES n/a COURSES n/a FELLOWSHIPS n/a PUBLICATIONS n/a

107. **Institute for Renaissance Interdisciplinary Studies (IRIS)**
HUM 223, State University of New York, Albany, NY 12222, USA
TEL n/a OFFICERS Dir. Prof. Raymond Ortali PUBLICATIONS "IRIS Newsletter" No longer extant

108. **Institute of Medieval Studies**
Katholieke Universiteit Leuven, Blijde-Inkomststraat 21, B-3000 Louvain, Belgium
TEL (016) 28–50–19 FAX (016) 28–50–25 OFFICERS Pres. Prof. J. de Smet; Secr. Dr. W. Verbeke FOUNDED 1966 MEMBERSHIP n/a AFFILIATION Faculty of Arts LIBRARY yes SPECIALIZATION Middle Ages HOURS n/a ANNUAL CLOSURE n/a RESEARCH INTERESTS n/a ACTIVITIES Seminars and colloquia. COURSES for 'Diploma' and Ph.D. in Medieval Studies FELLOWSHIPS nil SEE ALSO the Institut d'Etudes Médiévales at the Université Catholique de Louvain (since 1970 these two universities with the same name have in fact been independent) PUBLICATIONS *Mediaevalia Lovaniensia*

109. **Institute of Medieval Studies**
Université de Fribourg, CH-1700 Fribourg, Switzerland
TEL (0041) 37–21–93–72 OFFICERS Dir. Dr. P. Ladner, Dr. C. Pfaff, Dr. A. Schmid FOUNDED 1966 MEMBERSHIP n/a AFFILIATION Philosophische Fakultät der Universität Freiburg/Schweiz LIBRARY Bibliothek des Mediävistischen Instituts (ca. 4000 vols.) SPECIALIZATION Edition, Quellenkunde, Inschriften RESEARCH INTERESTS Edition von Inschriften, liturgischen texten, Landesgeschichte COURSES Vorlesungen im Rahmen der Philosophischen Fakultät FELLOWSHIPS nil PUBLICATIONS *Corpus inscriptionum Medii Aevi Helvetiae*; *Spicilegium Friburgense*

110. **Institut für europäische Geschichte**
Domus Universitatis, Alte Universitätstrasse 19, D-6500 Mainz, West Germany
TEL 0049–6131–224870 (Religionsgeschichte) 226143 (Universalgeschichte)
OFFICERS Dirs Prof. Dr. Peter Manns (Abt Religionsgeschichte); Prof. Dr.
K.O. von Aretin (Abt Universalgeschichte) FOUNDED 1950 MEMBERSHIP
n/a AFFILIATION ind. LIBRARY 160,000 vols SPECIALIZATION modern European and church history (Reformation) HOURS 8h30–13h00; 14h00–17h30. ANNUAL CLOSURE n/a RESEARCH INTERESTS modern European and church history, with a specialization in the Reformation ACTIVITIES
colloquia, seminars, lectures COURSES nil FELLOWSHIPS yes, stipendiary
and visiting fellowships. PUBLICATIONS *Veröffentlichungen*, vol. 1 (1952),
vol. 132 (1988); *Vortrage*, vol. 1 (1954), vol. 82 (1988); *Beihefte*, vol. 1 (1975),
vol. 25 (1988)

111. **Institut für mittelalterliche Realienkunde**
Körnermarkt 13, A-3500 Krems an der Donau, Austria
TEL 02732/4793 OFFICERS Dir. Univ. Prof. Dr. Harry Kühnel FOUNDED
1969 MEMBERSHIP n/a AFFILIATION Oesterr. Akademie der Wissenschaften LIBRARY 5,000 vols; 80 journals SPECIALIZATION daily life
and material culture of the Middle Ages HOURS 8h00–16h00; free admission ANNUAL CLOSURE nil RESEARCH INTERESTS social history of the
Middle Ages ACTIVITIES conferences, seminars, colloquia COURSES nil
FELLOWSHIPS nil PUBLICATIONS *Veröffentlichungen der Instituts für mittelalterliche Realienkunde Oesterreichs*, vol. 1 (1976) (irregular)

112. **Institut für Schweizerische Reformationgeschichte**
Rämistrasse 101, Universität Zürich, CH-8092 Zürich, Switzerland
No further information available at this time

113. **Institut für Spätmittelalter und Reformation**
Universität Tübingen, Hölderlinstrasse 17, D-7400 Tübingen, West Germany
TEL 07071–292886 OFFICERS Dir. Prof. Dr. Ulrich Köpf FOUNDED
1963 MEMBERSHIP n/a AFFILIATION Universität Tübingen, Evangelischtheologische Fakultät LIBRARY 3500 books; 10 journal subscriptions SPECIALIZATION Late Middle Ages, Renaissance, Reformation HOURS 9h00–16h00 ANNUAL CLOSURE n/a RESEARCH INTERESTS Late Middle Ages,
Renaissance, Reformation, Church History ACTIVITIES Seminars, conferences COURSES Study of Church History for university students FELLOWSHIPS nil PUBLICATIONS n/a

114. **Institut Interuniversitaire pour l'Etude de la Renaissance et de l'Humanisme (Instituut voor studie van de Renaissance en het Humanisme)**
Université Libre de Bruxelles, bd de la Plaine 2 (CP 240), B-1050 Bruxelles,
Belgium (or) Vrije Universiteit Brussel, Pleinlaan 2 (PF 240), B-1050 Bruxelles, Belgium

TEL (02) 641–2661 OFFICERS Hon.Dir. Prof. Em. Aloïs Gerlo; Dir. Prof. Pierre Jodogne FOUNDED 1960 MEMBERSHIP n/a AFFILIATION Université Libre de Bruxelles / Vrije Universiteit Brussel LIBRARY 1500 vols; 10 périodiques SPECIALIZATION Archives Correspondance Juste Lipse et Marnix de Ste Aldegonde HOURS n/a ANNUAL CLOSURE juillet-août RESEARCH INTERESTS Humanisme des anciens Pays-Bas; épistolographie humaniste; Erasmus; Marnix de Ste Aldegonde; Justus Lipsius; Beverland; etc. ACTIVITIES colloques triennaux COURSES nil FELLOWSHIPS nil PUBLICATIONS *Travaux de l'I.R.H.* (Actes des colloques); *Instrumenta Humanistica*; Collaboration à *La Correspondance d'Erasme* (12 vols); *Iusti Lipsi Epistolae*; *Bibliographie de l'Humanisme des Anciens Pays-Bas*; etc.

115. **Institute of Historical Research**
Senate House, Malet Street, London, WC1E 7HU, England
TEL (01) 636–0272–3 OFFICERS Dir. Prof. F.M.L. Thompson FOUNDED 1921 MEMBERSHIP n/a AFFILIATION University of London LIBRARY 136,000 items HOURS 9h00–21h00 Monday to Friday; 9h00–17h00 Saturday ACTIVITIES Anglo-American Conference of Historians (annual) COURSES yes, towards an M.A. in European Labour History. FELLOWSHIPS Research Fellowships in History for students completing their doctoral theses. No Stipendiary Visiting Scholarships PUBLICATIONS *Historical Research*, vol. 1 (formerly "Bulletin of the I.H.R."); *Fasti Ecclesiae Anglicanae* 1066–1300 (4 vols), 1300–1541 (12 vols), 1541–1857 (5 vols.); "Victorian History of the Counties of England" (182 vols to date)

116. **Instituto de História e Teoria das Ideias**
Faculdade de Letras, 3049 Coimbra Codex, Portugal
TEL 25551 OFFICERS Dir. Prof. Dr. Manuel Augusto Rodrigues FOUNDED n/a MEMBERSHIP n/a AFFILIATION Universidade de Coimbra LIBRARY 5,781 imprimés modernes SPECIALIZATION HOURS 9h00–17h00 lundi à vendredi ANNUAL CLOSURE n/a RESEARCH INTERESTS Il y a un champ de recherche sur l'Humanisme, la Réforme, et la Contre-Réforme. ACTIVITIES organisation occasionelle de séminaires, colloques, congrès. COURSES d'histoire culturelle et politique de l'Europe et du Portugal (siècles IIIe-XXe), dans le cadre de la Faculté de Lettres. FELLOWSHIPS on invite, parfois, des spécialistes à faire conférences et seminaires, avec traitement. PUBLICATIONS *Revista de História das Ideias*, vol. 1; "Diálogos com a História" (Séries)

117. **Instituto Português da Sociedade Científica de Görres**
Universidade Católica Portuguesa, Palma de Cima, 1600 Lisboa, Portugal
TEL (0351–1) 726–55–54 OFFICERS Co-dir. Prof. J. Bacelar e Oliveira; Prof. Dietrich Briesemeister FOUNDED 1962, by German Görres Scientific Society (Görres Gesellschaft zur Pflege der Wissenschaft) MEMBERSHIP n/a AFFILIATION Universidade Católica Portuguesa LIBRARY ca. 8,000 vols. SPE-

CIALIZATION 16th and 17th cent. literature, mainly Portuguese and Spanish, with particular emphasis on the works of F. António Vieira. HOURS 9h00–18h00, Monday to Friday; open to students and scholars upon presentation of student or identity card. ANNUAL CLOSURE August RESEARCH INTERESTS Portuguese studies; edition of rare literary texts; studies in the history of theology and philosophy, language, literature, culture, history, and society both in Portugal and in Brazil; the works of F. António Vieira. ACTIVITIES occasional conferences and seminars. COURSES nil FELLOWSHIPS nil EXTRACT FROM THE BROCHURE The Institute and Library have been entrusted to the care of the Portuguese Catholic University by an agreement (1980) with the German Görres Scientific Society. In November 1987 the Institute was moved to its present location, in the newly-built John Paul II University (same address as above) PUBLICATIONS "Portugiesische Forschungen der Görres-Gesellschaft" (3 series published by Verlag Aschendorff, Postfach 11 24, D-4400 Munich, West Germany)

118. **International Association for Neo-Latin Studies**
c/o Dept of English, College of Arts and Science, University of Rochester; Campus Station, Rochester, NY 14627, USA
OFFICERS Prof. Marjory Woods ACTIVITIES triennial congress; publication of proceedings. No further information available at this time

119. **Internationale Burckhardt Akademie**
piazza San Salvatore in Lauro 13, I-00186 Roma, Italie
TEL (Italie 39) (6) 687.97.37 ou 89.92.26 OFFICERS Pres. Prof. dr. Aurelio Tommaso Prete FOUNDED n/a MEMBERSHIP n/a AFFILIATION Elle dépend de la Accademia Internazionale per l'Unità Culturale LIBRARY ca. 3,000 vols.; beaucoup de mss HOURS 10h30–13h00; fermée le samedi après-midi et les jours de fête ANNUAL CLOSURE juillet et aôut RESEARCH INTERESTS études sur la Renaissance au 19e siècle; Jacob Burckhardt. ACTIVITIES séminaires, colloques, etc., specialement à l'ouverture et à la fermée de l'année d'études COURSES oui, programmes variées FELLOWSHIPS On invite des professeurs et personalités sans traitement; fait la concession des titres academiques et donne des prix PUBLICATIONS *La Voce*; *Bulletin Burckhardt*

120. **International Center of Medieval Art**
c/o The Cloisters, Ft Tryon Park, New York, NY 10040, USA
TEL n/a OFFICERS n/a FOUNDED 1956 MEMBERSHIP over 1000 individual and institutional members AFFILIATION n/a LIBRARY n/a RESEARCH INTERESTS art and civilization of the Middle Ages ACTIVITIES ICMA sponsors projects to catalogue Romanesque and Gothic sculpture in American collections; sessions at the annual Conference on Medieval Studies at Western Michigan University in Kalamazoo COURSES nil FELLOWSHIPS nil PUBLICATIONS *Gesta*, vol. 1 (1961) (2 p.a.); "IMCS Newsletter"; assorted publications

121. **International Courtly Literature Society, Canadian Branch**
Northrop Frye Hall 204, Victoria College, University of Toronto, Toronto, Canada M5S 1K7
TEL (416)-585–4429 OFFICERS Pres. Prof. Robert Taylor FOUNDED 1981 MEMBERSHIP 45 AFFILIATION ICLS LIBRARY nil RESEARCH INTERESTS All aspects of culture centring on courts, especially in the Medieval period. Literature, history, and the arts. ACTIVITIES triennal international conference; sessions at the Canadian Learned Societies Meeting COURSES nil FELLOWSHIPS nil PUBLICATIONS *Encomia* (journal, containing annual bibliography)

122. **International Machiavelli Society**
c/o Prof. Victor Santi, Dept of Foreign Languages, University of New Orleans, New Orleans, LA 70148, USA
TEL (504) 286–6657 OFFICERS Pres. Prof. Victor A. Santi; Vice-Pres. Prof. Edmund Jacobitti FOUNDED n/a MEMBERSHIP n/a AFFILIATION ind. LIBRARY nil RESEARCH INTERESTS Niccolò Machiavelli and related topics ACTIVITIES annual conference COURSES nil FELLOWSHIPS nil PUBLICATIONS *Machiavelli Studies*, vol. 1 ; proceedings

123. **International Shakespeare Association**
c/o The Shakespeare Centre, Henley Street, Stratford-upon-Avon, Warwickshire CV37 6QW, England
TEL (0789) 20–4016 OFFICERS Chair Dr. Ann Jennalie Cook; Vice-Chair Dr. Levi Fox FOUNDED 1973 MEMBERSHIP 500 AFFILIATION ind. LIBRARY nil; books received are deposited with the Shakespeare Centre (q.v.) RESEARCH INTERESTS Shakespeare ACTIVITIES International Congress every five years; occasional lectures at different academic meetings around the world COURSES nil FELLOWSHIPS nil PUBLICATIONS Occasional Papers; Proceedings of I.S.A. World Shakespeare Congresses held in 1976, 1981, and 1986

124. **International Society for the History of Rhetoric**
Villa Spelman, Via San Leonardo 13, I-50125 Firenze, Italy
No further information available at this time

125. **International Society for the Study of Medieval Theatre**
c/o Prof. J.-C. Aubailly, Université de Perpignan, Chemin de la Passio Vella; F-66025 Perpignan, France
TEL 003–67–63–1878 OFFICERS Pres. Prof. Jean-Claude Aubailly FOUNDED 1974 MEMBERSHIP 80 Membres. Droit 50 FF/année universitaire AFFILIATION Indépendants et groupes LIBRARY nil RESEARCH INTERESTS Théâtre ACTIVITIES conférence tous les trois ans PUBLICATIONS *European Medieval Theatre* (bulletin annuel)

126. **Istituto di Bibliografia Musicale**
c/o Biblioteca Nazionale, Viale Castro Pretorio 135, I-00185 Roma, Italy
TEL (06) 498–9536 OFFICERS Pres. Giancarlo Rostirolla; Membri Anna Pia
Sciolari, Maria Szpadrowska Svampa FOUNDED n/a MEMBERSHIP n/a AF-
FILIATION ind. LIBRARY mss, rare books, modern imprints SPECIALIZA-
TION music bibliography (mss) HOURS 10–13h, open to the public ANNUAL
CLOSURE August RESEARCH INTERESTS census and cataloguing of Ital-
ian music mss ACTIVITIES seminars, conferences, colloquia COURSES yes,
towards a degree FELLOWSHIPS n/a PUBLICATIONS n/a

127. **Istituto di Studi Rinascimentali**
Via Scienze 17, I-44100 Ferrara, Italy
TEL (0532) 33.227 or 76.00.02 E-MAIL (for A. Quondam) BITNET
G2MFEV42@ICINECA OFFICERS Dir Prof. Amedeo Quondam FOUNDED
1983 MEMBERSHIP n/a AFFILIATION ind. LIBRARY connected with
the Biblioteca Ariostea SPECIALIZATION history, literature, art, musicology
HOURS 9h00–19h00; reserved access ANNUAL CLOSURE no RESEARCH
INTERESTS interdisciplinary studies in the Renaissance ACTIVITIES confer-
ences, colloquia, seminars; publication of *Schifanoia* and assorted monographs.
COURSES nil FELLOWSHIPS nil PUBLICATIONS *Schifanoia*, Vol. 1 (1986)
(semestrale), vol. 3 (1987); "Newsletter" No. 1 (marzo 1988) (semestrale); assorted monographs

128. **Istituto "Domus Galileiana"**
Via S. Maria 26, I-56100 Pisa, Italy
TEL 2–3726 OFFICERS Pres. Prof. Vincenzo Cappelletti FOUNDED 1941
MEMBERSHIP n/a AFFILIATION Ministero per i Beni Culturali e Ambien-
tali LIBRARY yes (mss, books, and items relating to Galileo) SPECIALIZA-
TION Galileo HOURS n/a RESEARCH INTERESTS Galileo and the history
of science ACTIVITIES conferences, seminars, colloquia COURSES yes FEL-
LOWSHIPS yes PUBLICATIONS *Physis*, vol. 1 (1959) (4 p.a., journal on the
history of science)

129. **Istituto Ellenico di Studi Bizantini e Post-Bizantini**
Castello 3412, I-30122 Venezia, Italy
TEL (41 Venezia) 522–6581 OFFICERS Dir. Prof. Nikolaos M. Panayotakis;
Secr. Dr Sotirios Messinis FOUNDED 1951 MEMBERSHIP n/a AFFILIA-
TION ind. LIBRARY 15,000 vols (mss, rare books, modern imprints, journals);
archives, 200,000 documents regarding the ancient community of the Greek
Orthodox Church in Venice SPECIALIZATION Byzantine and Post-Byzantine
history and civilization; Latins in the Levant HOURS 9–12h30, 3h30–6h30; by
permit ANNUAL CLOSURE nil RESEARCH INTERESTS Latins in the Levant; history of the Greek Diaspora; history of Greek printing; Post-Byzantine
art. ACTIVITIES conferences, etc. COURSES nil FELLOWSHIPS stipendiary and non-stipendiary fellowships for graduate students and for scholars

PUBLICATIONS *Thesaurismata*, vol. 1 (annual); a series of monographs

130. **Istituto Ludovico Zorzi per le Arti dello Spettacolo**
Palazzo Strozzi, Piazza Strozzi, I-50123 Firenze, Italy
TEL (039) 276.0526 OFFICERS Pres. Prof. Cesare Molinari; Vice-Pres. Prof.
Marcello Fagiolo FOUNDED 1988 MEMBERSHIP ca. 100 AFFILIATION
Assessorato alla Cultura della Provincia di Firenze LIBRARY yes, with "Fototeca" and stage models RESEARCH INTERESTS Renaissance Italian theatre, especially research on its stage and settings; planning is underway for the creation of a Museum of Musical and Scenic Culture of the Urban Image of Florence and Tuscany during the Renaissance and the Baroque Era ACTIVITIES occasional seminars and conferences; exhibitions

131. **Istituto Nazionale di Studi sul Rinascimento**
Palazzo Strozzi, Piazza Strozzi, I-50123 Firenze, Italy
TEL (01139) 055–287728 OFFICERS Pres. Prof. Eugenio Garin (1985–88);
Vice-Pres. Giovanni Nencioni (1985–88); Librarian Cesare Vasoli (1985–88)
FOUNDED 1937, by Ministero Cultura Nazionale MEMBERSHIP no fee AFFILIATION ind. LIBRARY biblioteca (25,000 vols., 500 periodicals) and fototeca (50,000 photographs) SPECIALIZATION Italian Renaissance and European Renaissance HOURS 9h00–13h00 ANNUAL CLOSURE August RESEARCH INTERESTS Italian Renaissance ACTIVITIES conferences, colloquia, seminars COURSES yes; seminars in collaboration with universities FELLOWSHIPS yes PUBLICATIONS *Rinascimento*, Series I, vol. 1 (1950) 11
(1960); Series II, vol. 1 (1961) (annual); "Studi e Testi"; "Atti di Convegni";
"Quaderni di Rinascimento"; "Carteggi Umanistici"; volumes out of Collections (Carteggio di Michelangelo, Studio Fiorentino, etc.)

132. **Istituto Nazionale di Studi sul Rinascimento Meridionale**
via R. Falvo 10, I-80100 Napoli, Italy
OFFICERS Pres. Prof. Mario Santoro; Secr. Prof. Michele Cataudella
FOUNDED 1982 MEMBERSHIP L.25,000 fee AFFILIATION ind. LIBRARY
specializes on history, literature, philosophy, and art in the Kingdom of Naples
and in Southern Italy in the 16th century HOURS 9h00–13h00 ANNUAL CLOSURE August RESEARCH INTERESTS history, literature, philosophy, art,
urban studies COURSES specialization courses for Italian and foreign scholars
FELLOWSHIPS only for those enrolled in the specialization courses PUBLICATIONS *Quaderni*; texts, editions

133. **Istituto per la Storia dell'Arte Lombarda Dipartimento di Studi Medioevali, Umanistici, e Rinascimentali**
Palazzo Reale, Piazza Duomo 14, I-20122 Milano, Italy
TEL (02) 87–8475, 80–8026 OFFICERS Pres. Prof. Angelo Caloia; Dir. Prof.
Dott. Maria Luisa Gatti Perer FOUNDED 1967 MEMBERSHIP n/a AFFILIATION Università Cattolica del Sacro Cuore; also associated with the Kress

Foundation, New York LIBRARY yes, with slide and photograph collection SPECIALIZATION History of Art in Lombardy HOURS 9h00–13h00; 15h00–19h00 ANNUAL CLOSURE August RESEARCH INTERESTS Lombard art ACTIVITIES seminars, conferences, colloquia, courses, exhibitions COURSES on the Renaissance in Lombardy FELLOWSHIPS n/a PUBLICATIONS Collaboration with *Arte lombarda* (4 p.a.), ed. by Maria Luisa Gatti Perer (c/o Il Vaglio, Cultura Arte, via Vitruvio 39, Milano)

134. **Istituto Storico Germanico**
Via Aurelia Antica 391, I-00165 Roma, Italy
TEL n/a OFFICERS Dir. Prof. R. Elze FOUNDED 1888 LIBRARY 100,000 vols. RESEARCH INTERESTS medieval to modern history PUBLICATIONS *Quellen und Forschungen aus Italienischen Archiven und Bibliotheken*, vol. 1 (1898) vol. 68 (1988) present

135. **Istituto Storico Italiano per il Medioevo**
Palazzo Borromini, Piazza dell'Orologio 4, I-00186 Roma, Italy
TEL 654–2075 or 65–7059 OFFICERS Pres. Prof. Raffaello Morghen; Secr. Prof. Isa Sanfilippo Lori FOUNDED 1883 MEMBERSHIP n/a AFFILIATION n/a LIBRARY 40,000+ vols, 220 journals SPECIALIZATION the Middle Ages in Italy, esp. in Rome HOURS n/a ANNUAL CLOSURE n/a RESEARCH INTERESTS the Middle Ages in Italy, esp. in Rome ACTIVITIES publication of the above journal and series; conferences, colloquia, seminars COURSES through the "Scuola Storica Nazionale di Studi Medievali" FELLOWSHIPS n/a PUBLICATIONS *Bollettino dell'Istituto Storico Italiano per il Medioevo e Archivio Muratoriano*, vol. 1 (annual); "Studi Storici" (series); "Rerum Italicarum Scriptores" (series); "Fonti per la Storia d'Italia" (series); "Regesta Chartarum Italiae" (series); "Repertorium Fontium Historiae Medii Aevi" (series)

136. **Istituto Storico Italo-Germanico in Trento**
Via S. Croce 77, I-38100 Trento, Italy
TEL (0461) 98–1617 OFFICERS Dir. Prof. Paolo Prodi; Pres. Prof. Adam Wandruszka FOUNDED n/a MEMBERSHIP n/a AFFILIATION Istituto Trentino di Cultura LIBRARY 70,000 vols.; 350 journals; ca 1000 rare books SPECIALIZATION History of civil and ecclesiastical institutions, scientific, cultural, economic and social history of Germany and Italy. HOURS 8–12h, 14–18h; for scholars, upon presentation of a letter of introduction from a university administrator ANNUAL CLOSURE nil RESEARCH INTERESTS Italian and German history; European history from the foundation of the Holy Roman Empire to the Second World War ACTIVITIES two weeks of seminars each September COURSES nil FELLOWSHIPS for graduate students of Italian, German, or Austrian nationality for participation in the seminars; research fellowships (18 months) to Italian graduate students only PUBLICATIONS *Annali dell'Istituto Storico Italo-Germanico in Trento*, vol. 1 (1975); *Quaderni*; assorted monographs

137. **Kentron Erevnis Messeonikou kai Neou Ellinismou (Centre for Research into Medieval and Modern Hellenism)**
Akadimia Athinon, Odos Panepistimiou 28, Athens, Greece
TEL 361–4552 FOUNDED 1930 LIBRARY n/a RESEARCH INTERESTS n/a ACTIVITIES n/a COURSES n/a FELLOWSHIPS n/a PUBLICATIONS *Epetiris* (annual; 1958-present)

138. **Koninklijke Academie voor W., L. en S.K. van België (Royal Belgian Academy of Sciences, Letters, and Fine Arts)**
Paleis der Academiën, Hertogsstraat 1, B-1000 Brussel, Belgium
TEL (02) 511.2623 / 511.2629 OFFICERS Secr. Prof. Gerard Verbeke FOUNDED 1936MEMBERSHIP three classes of 30 members each, and 10 corresponding members. The Commission for the Study of Humanism of the Low Countries has four members of the Class of Letters and a varying number of associates (non-members of the Academy) LIBRARY yes SPECIALIZATION academic publications HOURS normal business hours RESEARCH INTERESTS Justus Lipsius, Humanism and Neo-Latin literature in the Low Countries COURSES nil FELLOWSHIPS nil PUBLICATIONS *Opus Epistolarum Iusti Lipsi*; Bibliographie de l'humanisme belge 1970–1985

139. **Lute Society of America**
c/o Prof. Victor Coelho, Dept of Music, University of Calgary, Calgary, Alberta, Canada T2N 1N4
TEL (403) 220–6990 OFFICERS Journal Editor Prof. Victor Coelho FOUNDED 1968 MEMBERSHIP 2500 AFFILIATION ind. LIBRARY nil RESEARCH INTERESTS Music, the lute instruments (iconography, analysis, archival studies) ACTIVITIES summer seminars PUBLICATIONS *Journal of the Lute Society of America* (annual); "Newsletter" (4 p.a.)

140. **Malone Society**
c/o Lois Potter, Dept of English, University of Leicester, Leicester, LE1 7RH, England
TEL (0533) 52.26.28 OFFICERS Gen. Ed. Dr John Pitcher (St John's College, Oxford); Treas. Mrs Leah Scragg (Dept of English, Univ. of Manchester); Chair Prof. Richard Proudfoot (King's College, London) LIBRARY nil RESEARCH INTERESTS the Society exists solely to publish editions and facsimiles of dramatic texts and related material in English, 1500–1642 COURSES nil FELLOWSHIPS nil PUBLICATIONS "Malone Society Reprints"; "Annual Report"

141. **Medieval and Renaissance Collegium (MARC)**
3405–07 Modern Languages Building, The University of Michigan, Ann Arbor, MI 48109–1275, USA
TEL (313) 763–2066 OFFICERS Dir. Prof. Guy Mermier FOUNDED n/a MEMBERSHIP n/a AFFILIATION University of Michigan LIBRARY min-

imal SPECIALIZATION Medieval and Renaissance Studies HOURS regular office hours; access through departmental office ANNUAL CLOSURE n/a RESEARCH INTERESTS Medieval and Renaissance Studies ACTIVITIES conferences, colloquia, seminars COURSES yes, towards a B.A. FELLOWSHIPS nil PUBLICATIONS MARC Monograph Series

142. **Medieval and Renaissance Drama Society**
c/o Prof. Martin Stevens, Dept of English, CUNY, Baruch College, New York, NY 10010, USA
TEL (418)-596–0372 OFFICERS Pres. Prof. Alexandra F. Johnston; Secr.-Treas. Prof. Milla Riggio (Trinity College, Hartford, CT 06105, USA) FOUNDED 1981, by David Berington (Pres. 1981–86) MEMBERSHIP 280 members; US$6/yr AFFILIATION MLA allied organization LIBRARY n/a RESEARCH INTERESTS n/a ACTIVITIES Annual Meeting at MLA COURSES nil FELLOWSHIPS nil PUBLICATIONS supports *Research Opportunities in Renaissance Drama (RORD)*

143. **Mediaeval and Renaissance Guild**
St John's College, University of Manitoba, Winnipeg, Canada R3T 2N2
TEL (204) 474–8519 OFFICERS Dir. L. Ritchey FOUNDED 1967 MEMBERSHIP n/a AFFILIATION University of Manitoba LIBRARY n/a RESEARCH INTERESTS n/a ACTIVITIES special research projects, conferences, symposia, lectures COURSES institutes study programmes, with 11 univ. depts co-operating FELLOWSHIPS n/a PUBLICATIONS n/a

144. **Medieval and Renaissance Studies Program University of Pittsburgh**
1328 C.L., University of Pittsburgh, Pittsburgh, PA 15260, USA
TEL (412) 624–6224 OFFICERS Dir Prof. Barbara N. Sargent-Baur FOUNDED 1968 MEMBERSHIP n/a AFFILIATION University of Pittsburgh LIBRARY nil, but uses the Hillman Library (univ. libr.) HOURS 7h50–24h00 Monday-Friday, 8h30–16h45 Saturday, 12h00–24h00 Sunday ANNUAL CLOSURE nil RESEARCH INTERESTS French, Italian, English, German, History, Art History, Religious Studies, History and Philosophy of Science. ACTIVITIES Sponsors an annual lecture series on topics in the Middle Ages and the Renaissance, a triennial symposium (rotating among Univ. of Pittsburgh, Penn. State Univ., and the Univ. of Pennsylvania) COURSES yes, at the undergraduate and graduate level, towards a Certificate in Medieval and Renaissance Studies FELLOWSHIPS available (at the graduate level) through the department of concentration PUBLICATIONS *Emblematica*, vol. 1 (1987) (biennial)

145. **Medieval Institute Notre Dame**
715 Hesburgh Library, Notre Dame, IN 46556, USA
TEL (219) 239–6603 or 239–6604 OFFICERS Dir. Prof. John Van Engen; Curator Prof. Lou Jordan FOUNDED 1952 MEMBERSHIP n/a AFFILIATION University of Notre Dame LIBRARY 60 mss; 200 rare books; 60,000 modern

imprints; 15,000 microforms (from the Biblioteca Ambrosiana, Milan); 340 journals SPECIALIZATION medieval intellectual history, history of universities. HOURS 8h00–23h45 Mon. to Fri., 9h00–23h45 Sat., 13h00–11h45 Sun. ANNUAL CLOSURE Christmas break (ca. 23 Dec. 2 Jan.) RESEARCH INTERESTS All aspects of Medieval Studies, esp. intellectual and religious history ACTIVITIES Annual conference COURSES yes, towards an MMS and Ph.D. in Medieval Studies FELLOWSHIPS Tuition Fellowships and Graduate Assistantships for graduate students. Small stipends for work in the Ambrosiana PUBLICATIONS "Publications in Mediaeval Studies" (ca. 30 vols. to date); "Texts and Studies in the History of Medieval Education" (17 vols.)

146. **Medieval Institute Southern Methodist University**
Dept of English, Southern Methodist University, Dallas, TX 75275, USA
No further information available at this time

147. **Medieval Institute Western Michigan University**
Western Michigan University, Kalamazoo, MI 49008, USA
TEL (616) 387–4145 FAX (616)-387–4150 OFFICERS Dir. Prof. Otto Gründler FOUNDED 1961 MEMBERSHIP n/a AFFILIATION Western Michigan University LIBRARY yes (extensive) SPECIALIZATION spec. coll. of Cistercian mss and incunabula; Italian reformers HOURS 8 am 11 pm ANNUAL CLOSURE open year round RESEARCH INTERESTS medieval culture, Renaissance, Reformation, history, theology, philosophy, etc. ACTIVITIES annual international conference; publications COURSES Undergraduate, Graduate (M.A.) degree programmes in Medieval Studies FELLOWSHIPS Graduate Fellowships, Graduate Assistantships; 1 annual fellowship for outside researchers for a period of 1–2 months (June/July) with no stipend; on-campus free apartment provided PUBLICATIONS *Medieval Prosopography* (2 issues per year); **Vox Mediaevalis** (annual newsletter) **Studies in Medieval Culture** (series); *Early Drama Art and Music (EDAM)* (monograph series and reference series); EDAM Newsletter (2 per year); Non-series volumes and Festschriften

148. **Medieval Studies**
Round Hall, Plymouth State College, Plymouth, NH 03264, USA
TEL (603) 536–5000 ext. 2425 OFFICERS Dir. Prof. Manuel Marquez-Sterling; Assist. Dir. Ms Robin Brodeur FOUNDED n/a MEMBERSHIP n/a AFFILIATION Plymouth State College LIBRARY yes (modern imprints, journals) SPECIALIZATION Middle Ages HOURS 8h00–22h00; open to the public ANNUAL CLOSURE some hours during vacation RESEARCH INTERESTS all aspects of the Middle Ages ACTIVITIES Annual "Medieval Forum" (now in its 10th year; a two-day conference with academic papers, concerts, displays) COURSES yes, towards a 4-year B.A. in Medieval Studies FELLOWSHIPS nil PUBLICATIONS nil

149. **Medieval Studies Centre**
Pontificia Università Salesiana, Piazza Ateneo Salesiano 1, 00139 Città del Vaticano, Vatican City
TEL (013) 2041 (univ.). No further information available at this time

150. **The H.H. Meeter Center for Calvin Studies**
Calvin College and Seminary, Grand Rapids, MI 49506, USA
TEL (616) 957–7081 OFFICERS Dir. Dr. Richard C. Gamble; Curator Peter De Klerk FOUNDED 1981 AFFILIATION Calvin College and Seminary LIBRARY 3,700 books; 12,500 articles; microfilms and microfiches RESEARCH INTERESTS Jean Calvin FELLOWSHIPS several fellowships available for students and scholars PUBLICATIONS *Calvin Theological Journal*; "Newsletter"; "Bibliotheca Calviniana"

151. **Mid-Atlantic Conference Renaissance Society of America**
c/o Prof. Lancelot K. Donaldson, 530 Williams Hall, University of Pennsylvania, Philadelphia, PA 19104, USA
AFFILIATION Renaissance Society of America. No further information available at this time

152. **Milton Society of America**
c/o English Department, Duquesne Universitym Pittsburgh, PA 15282, USA
TEL(412) 434–6420 OFFICERS Secr. Prof. Albert C. Labriola FOUNDED n/a MEMBERSHIP n/a AFFILIATION ind. LIBRARY The Milton Society Archive and Library at the University of Wisconsin-Madison houses all the Society records and proceedings SPECIALIZATION Milton studies HOURS n/a ANNUAL CLOSURE n/a RESEARCH INTERESTS Milton studies ACTIVITIES an annual dinner-meeting on 28 Dec. in the city where the M.L.A. has its convention. COURSES nil FELLOWSHIPS nil PUBLICATIONS *Annual Bulletin of the Milton Society of America* (booklet listing the members, their addresses, and works in progress), vol. 1

153. **New England Renaissance Conference**
Clark Art Institute, Williamston, MA 01267, USA
TEL n/a OFFICERS Dir. Prof. Samuel Y. Edgerton, Jr. No further information available at this time

154. **New York City Renaissance Club**
c/o Richard Harrier, 35 West 9th Street, New York, NY 10011, USA
AFFILIATION Renaissance Society of America RESEARCH INTERESTS all aspects of the Renaissance ACTIVITIES The Club has been inactive for several years

155. **North-Central Conference, Renaissance Society of America**
c/o Prof. Barbara Carman Garner, Dept of English, Carleton University, Ottawa, Canada K1S 5B6

TEL (613) 788–2315 E-MAIL NCCRSA@CARLETON.CA OFFICERS Co-ordinating Secr. Prof. Barbara Carman Garner AFFILIATION Renaissance Society of America FOUNDED 1960 MEMBERSHIP 125 LIBRARY nil RESEARCH INTERESTS Renaissance and Reformation COURSES nil FELLOWSHIPS nil ACTIVITIES Annual conference, alternating between the USA and Canada PUBLICATIONS co-sponsor of *Renaissance and Reformation / Renaissance et Reforme*

156. **Northern California Renaissance Conference**
c/o Winfried Schleiner, Dept of English, University of California, Davis, CA 95616, USA
No further information available at this time

157. **Oxford Historical Society**
38 Randolph Street, Oxford OX4 1XZ, England
TEL n/a OFFICERS Hon. Treasurer R.B. Peberdy FOUNDED n/a MEMBERSHIP n/a AFFILIATION ind. LIBRARY nil RESEARCH INTERESTS History of Oxford ACTIVITIES n/a COURSES nil FELLOWSHIPS nil PUBLICATIONS volumes of documents relating to the history of Oxford (colleges, university, and city)

158. **Pacific-Northwest Renaissance Conference Renaissance Society of America**
c/o Prof. Nathan Cogan, Dept of English, Portland State University, Portland, OR 97207, USA
TEL n/a OFFICERS Pres. Nathan Cogan; Tres. James Marino; Secr. Robert Schartz FOUNDED 1956 MEMBERSHIP ca. 80 AFFILIATION Renaissance Society of America, Canadian Society for Renaissance Studies LIBRARY nil RESEARCH INTERESTS mostly English literature, but also history, art history, modern languages ACTIVITIES annual meeting COURSES nil FELLOWSHIPS nil PUBLICATIONS nil

159. **Pennsylvania Renaissance Seminar**
c/o Dr. Georgianna Ziegler, Special Collections, Van Pel Library, University of Pennsylvania, 3420 Walnut Street, Philadelphia, PA 19104–6206, USA
TEL (215) 898–7552 OFFICERS Pres. Dr. Georgianna Ziegler; Secr. Prof. Ivy Corfis FOUNDED n/a MEMBERSHIP n/a AFFILIATION Univ. of Pennsylvania LIBRARY access to the Rare Book and Furness Shakespeare Libraries at the Univ. of Penn. SPECIALIZATION Shakespeare and Renaissance English drama; Aristotle, texts and commentaries; Elzevier imprints; Tasso; Ariosto; STC books; neo-Latin literature; 17th cent. Latin Americana; herbals; Golden Age Spanish drama HOURS 9h00–16h45 Mon. to Fri.; 10h00–16h45 the first Sat. of ea. month during term (call 215–898–7088 for further information) ANNUAL CLOSURE national holidays RESEARCH INTERESTS interdisciplinary studies primarily in history, art history, classics, English, French, Italian ACTIVITIES sponsors speakers, primarily drawn from its own mem-

bers, or visiting scholars (ca. 6 times p.a.). Lectures are usually in the late afternoon, followed by discussion and dinner COURSES nil FELLOWSHIPS nil PUBLICATIONS nil

160. **Petrarca-Institut**
Universität Köln, Universitätsstrasse 81, D-5 Köln-Lindenthal, West Germany OFFICERS Dir. Prof. Dr. Bernhard König and Prof. Dr. Eberhard Müller-Bochat FOUNDED 1930 AFFILIATION University of Cologne LIBRARY specializing on Italian literature, 1300–1600 RESEARCH INTERESTS Petrarch; Petrarchism; Renaissance Italian literature; Italo-Spanish literary influences; Italian and Portuguese travel literature regarding Japan (16th and 17th centuries); Florentine Neo-platonism

161. **Plainsong and Mediaeval Music Society**
46 Bond Street, Egham, Surrey TW20 0PY, England TEL (0784) 3–7252 OFFICERS Pres. H. Chadwick; Secr. D. Hiley; Chair D.H. Turner FOUNDED 1883 MEMBERSHIP n/a AFFILIATION n/a LIBRARY n/a RESEARCH INTERESTS to promote the study and appreciation of plainsong and mediaeval music ACTIVITIES n/a COURSES n/a FELLOWSHIPS n/a PUBLICATIONS n/a

162. **Pontifical Institute for Mediaeval Studies**
59 Queen's Park Crescent East, University of St Michael's College, University of Toronto, Toronto, Canada M5S 2C4 TEL (416) 926–1300 OFFICERS Acting Pres. Fr. E. Synan C.S.B. FOUNDED 1929 (Canada's oldest interdisciplinary research institute) MEMBERSHIP n/a AFFILIATION University of St Michael's College LIBRARY 71,000 vols (528 reels of archival material from 160 libraries) RESEARCH INTERESTS from the Middle Ages to the Renaissance ACTIVITIES n/a COURSES yes, leading to a Licentiate FELLOWSHIPS n/a PUBLICATIONS "President's Report" (annual); *Medieval Studies*, vol. 1 (annual); "Toronto Medieval Latin Texts"; "Estienne Gilson Series"; "Subsidia Mediaevalia"

163. **Princeton University Renaissance Studies Colloquium**
c/o Prof. Thomas P. Roche, Jr., Dept of English, Princeton University, Princeton, NJ 08544, USA TEL n/a OFFICERS Prof. Thomas P. Roche, Jr. No further information available at this time

164. **Program in Medieval-Renaissance Studies**
New College of University of South Florida, 5700 N. Tamiani Trail, Sarasota, FL 34243, USA TEL (813) 359–4380 OFFICERS Dir. Prof. Lee Daniel Snyder FOUNDED 1976 MEMBERSHIP 7 faculty AFFILIATION New College, University of South Florida LIBRARY access to the New College Library (ca. 170,000 vols) SPECIALIZATION none HOURS 8h00–23h00 ANNUAL CLOSURE nil

RESEARCH INTERESTS general ACTIVITIES Biennial New College Conference on Medieval-Renaissance Studies (next conference 8–10 March 1990) COURSES undergraduate courses leading to an Honours B.A. FELLOWSHIPS nil PUBLICATIONS nil

165. **Program in Renaissance Studies**
Whitney Humanities Center, 53 Wall Street, Box 2968 Yale Station, New Haven, CT 06520, USA
TEL (203) 432–0670 OFFICERS (as of 1987/88) Chairman Prof. George K. Hunter; Graduate Studies Prof. George de F. Lord; Undergraduate Studies Prof. Christina Malcomson FOUNDED n/a MEMBERSHIP n/a AFFILIATION Yale University LIBRARY 500 books SPECIALIZATION n/a HOURS 9h00–4h30, weekdays; access with key from the secretary ANNUAL CLOSURE July/August RESEARCH INTERESTS n/a ACTIVITIES course offerings, only COURSES towards a Renaissance major for the B.A.; Ph.D. FELLOWSHIPS stipends for admitted graduate students PUBLICATIONS nil

166. **Records of Early English Drama**
Victoria University, University of Toronto, Toronto, Canada M5S 1K7
TEL (416) 585–4504 OFFICERS Dir. Prof. Alexandra F. Johnston; Exec. Ed. Dr. Sally-Beth MacLean FOUNDED 1975 MEMBERSHIP nil AFFILIATION University of Toronto and Victoria University LIBRARY small, in-house reference library SPECIALIZATION Medieval and Renaissance English drama; bibliographies; guides to English Records Offices; paleographical guides HOURS by appointment RESEARCH INTERESTS Medieval and Renaissance English drama ACTIVITIES publications of "Records of Early English Drama"; occasional conferences and seminars COURSES nil FELLOWSHIPS nil PUBLICATIONS "Records of Early English Drama" (10 collections to date); *REED Newsletter* issue 1 (1976) semiannual

167. **Regroupement Interdisciplinaire de Recherches sur la Renaissance**
Université de Paris III, Paris, France
No further information available at this time

168. **Renaissance Centre**
Carleton University, Ottawa, Canada K1S 5B6
TEL (613) 231–6343 OFFICERS Dir. Prof. Donald A. Beecher (Dept of English) FOUNDED 1975 MEMBERSHIP n/a AFFILIATION Carleton University LIBRARY nil RESEARCH INTERESTS Drama ACTIVITIES occasional colloquia, seminars, lectures COURSES n/a FELLOWSHIPS n/a PUBLICATIONS "Carleton Renaissance Plays in Translation" (6 vols. to date)

169. **Renaissance Conference of Southern California**
c/o Center for Humanistic Studies, Claremont McKenna College, Claremont, CA 91711, USA
TEL (714) 621–8000 ext. 2759 or 3041 OFFICERS Pres. Wendy Furman; 1st

Vice-Pres. Ann Cruz; 2nd Vice-Pres. Eunice Have Howe; Secr.-Treas. Chris Forney FOUNDED n/a MEMBERSHIP Academic, independent, student AFFILIATION umbrella organization for Renaissance interests in S. Calif. LIBRARY nil RESEARCH INTERESTS all areas of Renaissance study ACTIVITIES annual Southwest regional conference COURSES nil FELLOWSHIPS nil PUBLICATIONS "Newsletter" (4 p.a.); *Renaissance Re-readings Intertext and Context* (University of Illinois Press, 1988)

170. **The Renaissance Institute**
c/o Sophia University, 7–1 Kioi-cho, Chiyoda-ku, Tokyo 102, Japan
TEL (03) 238–3822 OFFICERS Dir. Prof. Dr. Toyohiko Tatsumi; Vice-Chairman & Ed. Prof. Dr. Peter Milward FOUNDED 1972 (Renaissance Centre, 1984) MEMBERSHIP ca. 353; 4,000 yen/year AFFILIATION Sophia Univ. LIBRARY 3,000 vols. (400 English Recusant Literature, 1,500 Shakespeare) SPECIALIZATION English Lit. in the 16th and 17th centuries HOURS 9h00–17h00 (Mon.-Fri.); 9h00–12h00 Sat. ANNUAL CLOSURE on Sundays; one Saturday per month; all of August; from Dec. 24 to Jan. 6 RESEARCH INTERESTS n/a ACTIVITIES series of lectures three times a year (spring, autumn, winter); general meeting for 2 days in Sept (including symposium, special lectures, and social gathering) COURSES seminars on Renaissance literature, thought, and culture at the undergraduate and post-graduate level, but not towards a degree FELLOWSHIPS nil PUBLICATIONS *Renaissance Monographs*, 14 vols. (1974–88) (annual); *The Renaissance Bulletin*, 14 vols. (1974–88) (annual); *Runessansu Sousho* (= Series of Books on the Renaissance) 18 vols. (1975–88); (annual); "Renaissance News" 7 Nos. (1981–87) (annual)

171. **Renaissance English Text Society**
The Newberry Library, 60 West Walton Street, Chicago, IL 60610, USA
OFFICERS Secr.-Treas. J.M. Wells. No further information available at this time

172. **Renaissance Seminars of Chicago**
Division of Humanities, University of Chicago, 1050 E. 59th Street, Chicago, IL 60637, USA
TEL (312) 702–9899 OFFICERS Co-Chairs Prof. David Bevington, Prof. Richard Strier; Secr.-Treas. Prof. Christina Von Nolcken FOUNDED by Edward Lowinsky, Prof., Dept. of Music, U of Chicago MEMBERSHIP 136 members AFFILIATION Univ. of Chicago LIBRARY access to the Univ. of Chicago Library SPECIALIZATION n/a HOURS seven days a week, usually until midnight; apply at entrance for access ANNUAL CLOSURE n/a RESEARCH INTERESTS medieval and Renaissance topics across all disciplines literature, history, philosophy, history of art, of science, etc. ACTIVITIES 6 meetings p.a. COURSES nil FELLOWSHIPS nil PUBLICATIONS nil

173. **Renaissance Society of America**
     1161 Amsterdam Avenue, New York, NY 10027, USA
     TEL (212) 280–2318 OFFICERS Executive Dir. Margaret L. King; Pres. Gene
     Brucker FOUNDED 1954 MEMBERSHIP 2000 individuals, 1150 institutions
     AFFILIATION Columbia University, NY LIBRARY n/a HOURS 9–5 RE-
     SEARCH INTERESTS interdisciplinary studies on the Renaissance ACTIVI-
     TIES publication of *Renaissance Quarterly*, *Renaissance News and Notes*, pub-
     lication program, coordinator of group research projects, annual conferences
     COURSES nil FELLOWSHIPS n/a PUBLICATIONS *Renaissance Quarterly*,
     vol. 1 (1948) (4 p.a.); *Renaissance News and Notes* (newsletter)

174. **Renaissance Studies Program Yale University**
     P.O. Box 2968 Yale Station, Yale University, New Haven, CT 06520, USA
     OFFICERS Prof. Thomas M. Green. No further information available at this
     time

175. **Renaissance Studies Programme University of Toronto**
     c/o Victoria College, University of Toronto, Toronto, Canada M5S 1K7
     TEL (416) 585–4486 OFFICERS Co-ordinator Prof. Konrad Eisenbichler
     FOUNDED 1979 AFFILIATION Victoria College, Univ. of Toronto LIBRARY
     access to U. of Toronto libraries and to the library of the Centre for Reformation
     and Renaissance Studies (Victoria University) (q.v.) ACTIVITIES interdisci-
     plinary undergraduate teaching, occasional guest lectures, seminars, exhibitions,
     etc. COURSES undergraduate, leading to a B.A. with a Major or a Minor in
     Renaissance Studies FELLOWSHIPS nil PUBLICATIONS nil (staff publica-
     tions only)

176. **Richard III Society**
     c/o Morris G. McGee, Dept of English, Partridge Hall 466, Montclair State
     College, Upper Montclair, NJ 07043, USA
     OFFICERS Dir. Prof. Morris G. McGee FELLOWSHIPS annual predoctoral
     fellowship program to support projects centering on the life and times of King
     Richard III of England

177. **Rocky Mountain Medieval and Renaissance Association**
     c/o Dept of History, Social Science Building 215, University of Arizona, Tuc-
     son, AZ 85721, USA
     TEL (602) 621–1491 OFFICERS Head Prof. Michael Schaller FOUNDED n/a
     MEMBERSHIP n/a AFFILIATION Univ. of Arizona LIBRARY access to the
     university library, 3.7 million items HOURS 8h00–24h00 ANNUAL CLO-
     SURE nil RESEARCH INTERESTS general ACTIVITIES occasional semi-
     nars, conferences, colloquia COURSES nil FELLOWSHIPS nil PUBLICA-
     TIONS *Journal of the Southwest*, vol. 1

178. **Roma nel Rinascimento**
     c/o Istituto Storico Italiano per il Medioevo, Palazzo Borromini, Piazza

dell'Orologio 4, I-00186 Roma, Italy
TEL 654–2075 or 65.70.59 OFFICERS Dir. Massimo Miglio FOUNDED 1984 MEMBERSHIP 40 LIBRARY yes, specializing on the Renaissance in Rome HOURS 9h00–13h00, 16h00–19h00 ANNUAL CLOSURE August RE-SEARCH INTERESTS history, literature, art, urban studies, archives, etc. relative to Rome in the period 1350–1550 circa ACTIVITIES seminars, conferences COURSES special one-week course "Studio per le fonti della storia di Roma" (9–14 Oct. 1989) FELLOWSHIPS yes PUBLICATIONS "R.R. Bibliografia e Note" vol. 1 (1985) annual; "R.R. Inedita" (3 vols. to date); Conference proceedings

179. **Romansk Institut**
(**Institut d'Etudes Romanes**) Københavns Universitet, Njalsgade 78–80, DK-2300 Københavns, Denmark
TEL (01) 54–2211 OFFICERS p.t. Nils Soelberg FOUNDED n/a MEMBER-SHIP n/a AFFILIATION Copenhagen University LIBRARY 56,000 vols.; 120 pér. SPECIALIZATION n/a HOURS 9–16h30, lundi-vendredi; avec carte d'étudiant ANNUAL CLOSURE juillet RESEARCH INTERESTS tout sujet situé à l'intérieur des langues, littératures, civilisations des pays de langue romane ACTIVITIES colloques, congrès occasionnelles COURSES oui; 1. cycle (équiv. DEUG), 2. cycle (Capes/mâitrise, sans concours); (1. et 2. cycle = 4 ans) FELLOWSHIPS oui PUBLICATIONS *Revue Romane* (2 p.a.); *Romansk Bibliotek*, vol. 1 (Série en danois); RIDS, publications internes des travaux en cours

180. **Seminar on Women in the Renaissance and Reformation**
c/o Center for Literary and Cultural Studies, Harvard University, Boston, Mass., USA
TEL (617) 495–0738 OFFICERS Elizabeth H. Hageman; Ann Rosalind Jones ACTIVITIES monthly meetings

181. **Seminarium Philologiae Humanisticae**
Faculteit der Letteren en Wijsbegeerte, Blijde Inkomsstraat 21, B-3000 Leuven, Belgium
TEL (32 Belgium) (16 Leuven) 285019 or 285022 OFFICERS Dir. Prof. Dr. Jozef IJsewijn; Assist. Dir. Dr. Gilbert Tournoy FOUNDED 1963 MEMBER-SHIP n/a AFFILIATION Katholieke Universiteit Leuven LIBRARY ca. 5000 vols.; 150 rare books; 100 microforms; 20 journals; the collection is also part of the university library SPECIALIZATION Humanism and Neo-Latin literature HOURS 9–19h; admittance with a reader's card from the univ. library ANNUAL CLOSURE week between Christmas and New Year RESEARCH INTERESTS Neo-Latin language and literature, with focus on Rome and the Netherlands ACTIVITIES Congress of Neo-Latin Studies; occasionally conferences of the Institute for Mediaeval Studies COURSES only within the Faculty Programme, at the graduate level in philology, history, and theology. Pro-

gramme offers 3 courses 1) History of Neo-Latin literature; 2) Study of a Neo-Latin author; and 3) History of Humanism FELLOWSHIPS not directly, but through the appropriate service of the university "Dienst Internationale Samenwerking", Oude Markt 13, B-3000 Leuven. tel. (32)(16) 284025 (students and accommodation) and 284027 (programs) PUBLICATIONS *Humanistica Lovaniensia*, since vol. 17 (1968) (annual) (Journal of Neo-Latin Studies); *Supplementa Humanistica Lovaniensia* (series) irregular. 5 vols (1978, 1979, 1981, 1986, 1990) to date

182. **Senatskommission für Humanismusforschung der Deutschen Forschungs-gemeinschaft**
Roter Graben 10, D-355 Marburg an der Lahn, West Germany
TEL n/a OFFICERS Pres. Rudolf Schmitz PUBLICATIONS *Mitteilungen* (12 vols. to date) ACTIVITIES conferences

183. **Shakespeare Association of America**
6328 Station B, Vanderbilt University, Nashville, TN 37235, USA
TEL (615) 794–9578 OFFICERS Pres. Anne Lancashire; Exec. Secr. Nancy Elizabeth Hodge FOUNDED 1973 MEMBERSHIP 850 AFFILIATION ind. LIBRARY nil RESEARCH INTERESTS drama of Shakespeare and his contemporaries in England; Shakespeare's verse ACTIVITIES annual conferences COURSES nil FELLOWSHIPS nil PUBLICATIONS *Bulletin of the Shakespeare Association of America*, vol. 1 (1978) (2 times p.a.)

184. **Shakespeare Centre**
Henley Street, Stratford-upon-Avon, Warwickshire CV37 6QW, England
TEL (0789) 20–4016 OFFICERS Dir. Dr Levi Fox, O.B.E.; Senior Librarian Mrs Marian J. Pringle; Senior Archivist Dr. Robert Bearman FOUNDED Shakespeare Birthplace Trust founded 1847 MEMBERSHIP Use of the Shakespeare Centre Library facilities is free to any 'bona fide' student or scholar AFFILIATION ind. LIBRARY ca. 40,000 vols (10,000 mss; 500 rare books; 100 modern imprints; 500 microforms; 20,000 photographs; 50 journals); a Records Office, with its own reading room, is attached to the library SPECIALIZATION Shakespeare, theatre, Warwickshire history and topography. Includes the Royal Shakespeare Theatre Library collections HOURS 10h00–17h00 weekdays; 9h30–12h30 Sat. ANNUAL CLOSURE bank holidays and Saturdays preceding bank holidays RESEARCH INTERESTS Shakespeare, the Elizabethan world, theatre, local studies. ACTIVITIES colloquia, seminars, exhibitions, conferences. Shakespeare Centre is admin. office for International Shakespeare Association COURSES a variety of courses for senior school students, interested individuals, degree students, etc., arranged on request or as part of the regular programme of the Centre's work FELLOWSHIPS nil. The Jubilee Educational Fund can assist scholars with small financial assistance; details available on written request to the Director EXTRACT FROM THE BROCHURE The Centre provides accommodation and facilities for the Trust's

educational activities, together with a visitors' centre for Shakespeare's Birthplace. The tasks of the Trust are to preserve and maintain the Shakespearean properties and to be responsible for assisting the general advancement of Shakespearean knowledge PUBLICATIONS guidebooks to Shakespeare properties; Levi Fox, *In Honour of Shakespeare* (Norwich, 1983)

185. **Shakespeare Institute**
Westmere, 50 Edgbaston Park Road, Birmingham B15 2RX, England (or) Mason Croft, Church Street, Stratford-upon-Avon CV37, England
TEL (021) 414–6202/3 (Birmingham) and (0789) 293138 (Stratford) OFFICERS Dir. Prof. Stanley Wells; Deputy Dir. Dr. T.P. Matheson; Librarian Dr. S.L. Brock FOUNDED 1951, by the University of Birmingham MEMBERSHIP Institute staff and registered students AFFILIATION University of Birmingham LIBRARY 120,000 vols (2500 rare books; 54,000 modern imprints 60,000 vol. equivalents in microform; 70 journals) SPECIALIZATION English dramatic literature, 1475–1700 HOURS 9–17h00 weekdays; access by application to the Director ANNUAL CLOSURE bank holidays and university closures RESEARCH INTERESTS textual, theatrical, and critical history of Shakespeare's plays; semiotics of text and performance; intellectual background to Renaissance literature ACTIVITIES Biennial International Shakespeare Conference; summer schools and short courses for undergraduates, graduates, and the general public COURSES yes, towards an M.A., M.Phil., Ph.D. FELLOWSHIPS may be available in future years PUBLICATIONS "Report of the International Shakespeare Conference" (proceedings); *Shakespeare Survey* (edited by the Director)

186. **Shelby Cullom Davis Center for Historical Studies**
Princeton University, Princeton, NJ 08544, USA
TEL n/a OFFICERS Dir. Prof. Lawrence Stone. No further information available at this time

187. **Sixteenth Century Studies Conference**
Laughlin Building 115, Northeast Missouri State University, Kirksville, MO 63501, USA
TEL (816) 785–4665 OFFICERS Secr. Robert V. Schnucker FOUNDED 1968 MEMBERSHIP 1200 individuals AFFILIATION ind.   LIBRARY nil RESEARCH INTERESTS anything having to do with early modern history (1450–1648) ACTIVITIES an annual conference (last weekend of October) COURSES nil FELLOWSHIPS three prizes for articles that have been or will be published the Carl Meyer Prize; the Grimm Prize; the Roelker Prize. All three prizes have monetary rewards and the first has the chance to appear in print. PUBLICATIONS *Sixteenth Century Journal*, vol. 1 (1970) (4 p.a.); *Sixteenth Century Essays & Studies; Historians of Early Modern Europe*

188. **Società di Studi Valdesi**
Via Roberto D'Azeglio 2, I-10066 Torre Pellice (Torino), Italy
No further information available at this time

189. **Società Italiana del Flauto Dolce**
Via Confalonieri 5, I-00195 Roma, Italy
TEL (06) 35–4441 OFFICERS Pres. Giancarlo Rostirolla (1971) FOUNDED
1971 MEMBERSHIP 2000 (lire 30,000; ca. US$24) AFFILIATION ind. LI-
BRARY modern imprints and facsimiles, journals, musical scores SPECIAL-
IZATION Renaissance and baroque music and instruments HOURS 9–16h,
open to the public, 3 days a week ANNUAL CLOSURE July-August RE-
SEARCH INTERESTS instrumental music of the Renaissance and Baroque
ACTIVITIES summer school (Urbino), journal, music school, occasional sem-
inars and master classes COURSES international course on early music (in
Urbino); a diploma is given at end of course. Music school at Centre in Rome;
from beginners to advanced FELLOWSHIPS nil PUBLICATIONS *Il Flauto
Dolce*, anno 1 (1971) (irregular to 1983, thereafter biannual); "Musiche da
suonare" and "Armonia Strumentale" (music series); proceedings from conferences

190. **Societas Internationalis Studiis Neolatinis Provehendis**
Institut d'Etudes Latins, rue Victor-Cousin 1, F-75230 Paris, France
OFFICERS Prof. Alain Michel. No further information available at this time

191. **Société de l'Histoire du Protestantisme Français**
54 rue des Saint-Pères, F-75007 Paris, France
TEL 45–48–6207 OFFICERS Pres. Jacques Bompaire (1985–89) FOUNDED
1852 MEMBERSHIP 40 AFFILIATION ind. LIBRARY Bibliothèque du
Protestantisme Français SPECIALIZATION 180,000 books from the 16th-
18th centuries; manuscripts, journals, etc. HOURS 14h00–18h00, Tuesday
through Saturday ANNUAL CLOSURE August RESEARCH INTERESTS
Reformation in France ACTIVITIES lectures, exhibits, seminars, conferences
COURSES nil FELLOWSHIPS nil PUBLICATIONS *Bulletin de la Société de
l'Histoire du Protestantisme Français* (4 p.a.)

192. **Société des Amis de Montaigne**
B.P. 92, Saint Mour, France
OFFICERS Prof. Robert Aulotte (6 La Garemme, 78120 Rombouillet, France)
FOUNDED 1913 MEMBERSHIP cotisation FF. 180/an AFFILIATION indép.
LIBRARY nil RESEARCH INTERESTS Montaigne et son temps COURSES
nil FELLOWSHIPS nil

193. **Société des Amis de Ronsard du Japon (SARJ)**
c/o Isamu Takata, 4–9–5 Isogo, Isogo-ku, Yokohama 235, Japan
TEL (045) 751–5286 OFFICERS Pres. Isamu Takata (1965–); Secr. gen. Fu-
miko Kigasawa (1986–); Treas. Yoshiko Aida (1987–88) FOUNDED 1965,

par Isamu Takata et ses élèves MEMBERSHIP 30 AFFILIATION ind. LI-BRARY nil RESEARCH INTERESTS Ronsard; littérature et culture de la Renaissance ACTIVITIES journées d'études annuelles; séminaires (occasionnellement), réunions d'étude mensuelles COURSES nil FELLOWSHIPS nil PUBLICATIONS *Revue des amis de Ronsard*, vol. 1 (May 1988) (annuel)

194. **Société d'Etude du XVIIe Siècle**
c/o Collège de France, 11 Place Marcelin-Berthelot, CCP 6511–05 D Paris, F-75231 Paris Cedex 05, France
TEL (1) (45) 48–8524 OFFICERS Pres. J. Truchet (1986) FOUNDED 1948 MEMBERSHIP 1250 AFFILIATION ind. LIBRARY nil RESEARCH INTERESTS XVIIe siècle; littérature; histoire, arts; philosophie. ACTIVITIES deux colloques par an (en mars et en octobre) COURSES nil FELLOWSHIPS nil PUBLICATIONS *XVIIe Siècle*, vol. 1 (4 p.a.)

195. **Société d'Etudes Latines de Bruxelles**
18 av. Van Cutsem, B-7500 Tournai, Belgium
TEL n/a OFFICERS Pres. M. Renard; Mme. J. Dumortier-Bibaum FOUNDED 1937 MEMBERSHIP ca. 750 AFFILIATION ind. LIBRARY nil RESEARCH INTERESTS toutes les publications concernant les études latines PUBLICATIONS *Latomus* (Revue d'études latines), vol. 1 (1941) (4/year); *Collection Latomes* (travaux, textes et éditions, traductions)

196. **Société Française des Seizièmistes**
1 rue Victor Cousin, F-75230 Paris Cedex 05, France
TEL n/a OFFICERS Dir. Prof. Claude Longeon; Conseil d'administration de 15 membres FOUNDED 1978 MEMBERSHIP 450 AFFILIATION ind. LI-BRARY nil RESEARCH INTERESTS Renaissance européenne, XVe-XVIIe siècles ACTIVITIES colloque annuel COURSES nil FELLOWSHIPS nil PUB-LICATIONS *Nouvelle Revue du XVIe Siècle*, vol. 1 (1983) (annuel); Actes des rencontres annuelles

197. **Société Internationale de Recherces Interdisciplinaires sur la Renaissance (S.I.R.I.R.)**
1 rue Victor Cousin, F-75230 Paris Cedex 05, France
TEL n/a OFFICERS Dir. Marie-Thèrese Jones-Davies FOUNDED n/a MEM-BERSHIP n/a AFFILIATION ind. LIBRARY oui, ca. 500 vols. HOURS n/a ANNUAL CLOSURE n/a RESEARCH INTERESTS n/a ACTIVITIES deux colloques par année universitaire COURSES Diplomes d'Etudes approfondis et thèse chez le Centre (qui existe encore pendant 5 ans, bien que la société ait une durée illimitée) FELLOWSHIPS oui, mais sans traitement PUBLICA-TIONS un volume annuel publié chez Jean Touzot Libraire-Editeur (Paris) sur le thème des colloques annuels

198. **Society for Medieval Archaeology**
c/o University College, Gower Street, London WC1, England
TEL n/a OFFICERS Pres. H.R. Loyan; Secr. H. Clarke FOUNDED 1957 MEM-
BERSHIP 1,800 AFFILIATION n/a LIBRARY n/a RESEARCH INTERESTS
n/a ACTIVITIES n/a COURSES n/a FELLOWSHIPS n/a PUBLICATIONS
Medieval Archaeology, vol. 1 (annual); Monograph Series

199. **Society for Post-Medieval Archeology, Ltd**
Council for British Archaeology, 112 Kensington Road, London, SE11 6RE,
England
TEL (01) 600–3699 OFFICERS Pres. Hugh Tait (1988); Secr. Mrs R. Wein-
stein (The Museum of London, London Wall, London EC2Y 5HN); Treas. P.J.
Davey Esq. (Dept of Continuing Education, 19 Abercromby Square, P.O. Box
147, Liverpoo L69 3BX) FOUNDED 1967 MEMBERSHIP 880 AFFILIATION
Council for British Archaeology, SHA LIBRARY nil RESEARCH INTER-
ESTS British and Colonial archaeology from the Middle Ages to the advent
of industrialization. ACTIVITIES biennial weekend conferences. COURSES
n/a FELLOWSHIPS n/a PUBLICATIONS *The Journal of the Society for Post
Medieval Archaeology*, vol. 1 (annual); Newssheet (2 p.a.)

200. **Society for Reformation Research**
6477 San Bonita Ave., St Louis, MO 63105, USA
FOUNDED 1947 MEMBERSHIP dues US$10 p.a. AFFILIATION Centre for
Reformation Research (q.v.)

201. **Society for Renaissance Studies**
c/o Dr Letizia Panizza, Royal Holloway and Bedford New College, University
of London, Egham Hill, Egham, Surrey TW 20 0EX, England
TEL n/a OFFICERS Chairman Prof. Sydney Anglo; Hon. Secr. Dr. Letizia
Panizza FOUNDED 1967 MEMBERSHIP 550 AFFILIATION ind. LIBRARY
nil RESEARCH INTERESTS all aspects of Renaissance studies ACTIVITIES
colloquia (2 or 3 p.a.); annual lecture in January; occasional conferences
COURSES nil FELLOWSHIPS nil PUBLICATIONS *Journal of Renaissance
Studies*, vol. 1 (March, 1987) (2 p.a.); *Bulletin*, vol. 1 (March, 1982) (2 p.a.),
sent to all members

202. **Society for the Study of Medieval Languages and Literature**
School of English, Leeds University, Leeds, England
TEL n/a OFFICERS Pres. Elspeth Kennedy; Vice-Pres. Norman Davis, Roger
Highfield, Sir Richard Southern; Secr. Charlotte Brewer (All Souls' Col-
lege, Oxford); Treas. D.G. Pattison (Magdalen College, Oxford); Ed. A.V.C.
Schmidt (Balliol College, Oxford); Assist. Ed. Jennifer Fellows FOUNDED
1932 MEMBERSHIP n/a AFFILIATION ind. LIBRARY nil RESEARCH
INTERESTS Medieval language and literature ACTIVITIES publication of
Medium Ævum COURSES nil FELLOWSHIPS nil PUBLICATIONS *Medium*

Ævum, vol. 1 (2 p.a.); occasional monographs

203. **South-Central Renaissance Conference**
c/o Donald R. Dickson, Dept of English, Texas A&M University, College Station, TX 77843, USA
TEL (409) 845–8340 OFFICERS Pres. Jay Anglin (Univ. of Southern Mississippi); Exec. Secr.-Treas. Donald R. Dickson FOUNDED n/a MEMBERSHIP n/a AFFILIATION ind. LIBRARY nil RESEARCH INTERESTS interdisciplinary research on the Renaissance ACTIVITIES annual conference COURSES nil FELLOWSHIPS one stipend p.a. to support the research of a SCRC member PUBLICATIONS *Explorations in Renaissance Culture*, vol. 1

204. **South-Eastern Renaissance Conference**
c/o Henry E. Jacobs, Dept of English, University of Alabama. P.O. Box AL University, AL 35486, USA
OFFICERS Chair Prof. Henry E. Jacobs. No further information available at this time

205. **Southern-California Renaissance Conference**
c/o Wendy A. Furman, Dept of English, Whittier College, Whittier, CA 90608, USA
TEL n/a OFFICERS Pres. Wendy A. Furman (Whittier College); Vice-Pres. Anne J. Cruz (Univ of Calif); 2nd Vice-Pres. Eunice Howe (Univ of S. Calif); Secr.-Treas. Kristine Forney (Calif State) FOUNDED ca. 1963 MEMBERSHIP 350 (US$10) AFFILIATION Huntington Library LIBRARY use of the Huntington Library PUBLICATIONS Newsletter (2 p.a.); Supported *Renaissance Rereadings Intertext and Context*, M.C. Horowitz, A.J. Cruz, and W.A. Furman, co-editors (Urbana, 1988) ACTIVITIES host annual southwest regional conference, symposia COURSES nil FELLOWSHIPS nil

206. **Spenser Society**
c/o Dept of English, 231 Arts and Science, University of Missouri, Columbia, MO 65211, USA
TEL (314) 882–3882 OFFICERS Pres. Judith Anderson; Secr.-Treas. Russell Meyer FOUNDED n/a MEMBERSHIP 150 (US$5) AFFILIATION ind. LIBRARY nil RESEARCH INTERESTS Edmund Spenser and related topics. ACTIVITIES sessions in conjunction with MLA and the International Congress on Medieval Studies at Western Michigan University, Kalamazoo (co-sponsored with "Spenser at Kalamazoo") COURSES nil FELLOWSHIPS nil PUBLICATIONS nil

207. **Thomas Morus Gesellschaft**
Hubertushöhe 9, Bensberg, D-5060 Bergisch Gladbach 1, West Germany
TEL 02204–54607 OFFICERS Dr. Hermann Boventer; Msgr. Josef Seuffer; Dr. Theo Hermes FOUNDED 1980 MEMBERSHIP 420 AFFILIATION Amici Thomae Mori LIBRARY n/a RESEARCH INTERESTS Thomas More, Renais-

sance Studies, Humanism ACTIVITIES Two annual seminars, each one week; Conferences; talks; exhibitions; Thomas-More-Medal annually to a person of public standing COURSES nil FELLOWSHIPS nil PUBLICATIONS *Thomas-Morus-Jahrbuch*, vol. 1 (1981)

208. **Toronto Renaissance and Reformation Colloquium**
c/o CRRS, Victoria University, University of Toronto, Toronto, Canada M5S 1K7
TEL (416) 585–4484 or 585–4468 OFFICERS Chairman Prof. Massimo Ciavolella (1989–90); Vice-Chairman Prof. Erika Rummel (1989–90) FOUNDED 1964 MEMBERSHIP ca. 130 AFFILIATION ind. LIBRARY nil RESEARCH INTERESTS all aspects of the Renaissance and/or Reformation ACTIVITIES annual lecture series (6 p.a.), triennial conference. COURSES nil FELLOWSHIPS nil PUBLICATIONS co-sponsor of *Renaissance and Reformation / Renaissance et Reforme*

209. **Villa I Tatti**
The Harvard University Center for Italian Renaissance Studies
Via di Vincigliata 26, I-50135 Firenze, Italy
TEL (055) 603.251 OFFICERS Dir. Prof. Walter Kaiser (since July 1988); Research Librarian Dr. Julian Kliemann FOUNDED 1961; the villa is the former residence of Bernard Berenson MEMBERSHIP n/a AFFILIATION Harvard University LIBRARY Biblioteca Berenson (80,000 vols.; c. 400 periodicals; 200,000 photographs) SPECIALIZATION Italian history, literature, art and music in the Renaissance HOURS 9h00–18h00 ANNUAL CLOSURE August RESEARCH INTERESTS all aspects of the Italian Renaissance, but esp. the history of art. ACTIVITIES conferences, seminars, occasional colloquium COURSES nil FELLOWSHIPS 10 or more stipendiary fellows PUBLICATIONS *I Tatti Studies*, vol. 1 (1985) (annual); vol. 2 (1987)

210. **Warburg Institute**
Woburn Square, London WC1H 0AB, England
TEL (01) 580–9663 OFFICERS Dir. Prof. J.B. Trapp; Secr. and Registrar Miss A.C. Pollard; Librarian Dr. W.F. Ryan FOUNDED 1904 MEMBERSHIP n/a AFFILIATION Univ. of London LIBRARY Institute's archives; 250,000 rare and modern books and pamphlets; 300,000 photographs; 250 microforms; 2,000 journals. SPECIALIZATION cross-disciplinary cultural and intellectual history of Europe, the Near and Middle East, and to some extent the Far East, with special reference to the afterlife of Greco-Roman Antiquity HOURS 10h00–18h00, Monday to Friday; 10h00–13h00 Saturday. Access for staff from other learned institutions is by letter of identification; for graduate students by letter of recommendation from a supervisor or adviser; others, by writing in advance to the Director ANNUAL CLOSURE one week at Easter, and one at Christmas RESEARCH INTERESTS see above under LIBRARY SPECIALIZATION ACTIVITIES colloquia, conferences, seminars COURSES postgraduate study

by course work and thesis (M.Phil. degree in Combined Historical Studies), or by thesis alone (M. Phil. and Ph.D) FELLOWSHIPS long term (1–3 years) and short-term (1–3 months), Frances A. Yates Fellowships for younger scholars under 35 who have completed at least 2 years' graduate study PUBLICATIONS *Journal of the Warburg and Courtauld Institutes*, vol. 1 (1937) (annual); *Studies of the Warburg Institute*; *Warburg Institute Surveys and Texts*; *Oxford-Warburg Studies*; *Corpus Platonicum Medii Aevi*; *Medieval and Renaissance Studies*

211. **Werkgroep Engels-Nederlandse Betrekkingen / Sir Thomas Browne Institute**

P.O. Box 9515, 2300 RA Leiden, The Netherlands
TEL (071) 27–2155 or 27–2144 OFFICERS Chairman J. van den Berg (Dept of Church History); Secr. P.G. Hoftijzer FOUNDED 1961 MEMBERSHIP open; no fee AFFILIATION Rijksuniversiteit te Leiden LIBRARY small collection of books SPECIALIZATION Anglo(-Amer.)-Dutch cultural relations, 16th-18th cent. HOURS n/a ANNUAL CLOSURE n/a RESEARCH INTERESTS Anglo(-Amer.)-Dutch cultural relations, 16th-18th century ACTIVITIES publication of the above series COURSES M.A. courses on Anglo-Dutch relations FELLOWSHIPS no fellowships can be offered, but residence of outside researchers to work at the Institute is possible EXTRACT FROM BROCHURE the Werkgroep/Institute continues and extends the activities of the original Sir Thomas Browne Institute which was founded in 1960. In its present form it is an interdisciplinary research unit of the University of Leiden consisting of scholars from the departments of English, Dutch History, Art History, and Church History, and a number of affiliated scholars from other institutions. The Institute is a research centre rather than an 'institute' in the accepted sense of the word. It does not offer fellowships or ample office space to visitors from abroad, although it is always glad to assist scholars working in the same field. It does not have specialized library facilities, but the rich collections of the Leiden University Library are housed next door to it in the new Arts Centre PUBLICATIONS "Publications of the Sir Thomas Browne Institute" (series, published through E.J. Brill and the Leiden University Press); Publication of annual symposium papers

212. **West Virginia Shakespeare and Renaissance Association**

c/o Sophia B. Blaydes, Department of English, West Virginia University, Morgantown, WV 26506, USA
TEL (304) 293–3107 OFFICERS Treas. Prof. Sophia Blaydes; (other officers rotate) FOUNDED n/a MEMBERSHIP n/a AFFILIATION ind. LIBRARY nil RESEARCH INTERESTS any aspect of Shakespeare and Renaissance culture ACTIVITIES annual conference and occasional colloquia COURSES nil FELLOWSHIPS nil PUBLICATIONS *Selected Papers from the West Virginia Shakespeare and Renaissance Association*

213. **Wolfenbüttler Arbeitskreis für Renaissance**
Herzog August Bibliothek, Wolfenbüttler, West Germany
TEL n/a OFFICERS Dir. Dr. August Buck PUBLICATIONS *Wolfenbüttler Renaissance Mitteilungen*; "Wolfenbüttler Abhandlungen zur Renaissance-forschung" (5 vols. to date). No further information available at this time

Addendum

214. **Society for Confraternity Studies**
c/o Prof. Kathleen Falvey, Dept of English, University of Hawaii at Manoa, Honolulu, HW 96822, USA
TEL: (808) 948)8802 OFFICERS: Pres.: Prof. Kathleen Falvey FOUNDED: 1989 MEMBERSHIP: n/a AFFILIATION: ind. LIBRARY: a special collection is being assembled at the Centre for Reformation and Renaissance Studies, Toronto (q.v.) from publications donated by members of the society and other interested scholars; for further information contact the Centre for Reformation and Renaissance Studies PUBLICATIONS: *Confraternitas* 1 (1990) (2 p.a.); for information contact K. Eisenbichler or W.R. Bowen, CRRS, Victoria College, U. of Toronto, Toronto, Canada M5S 1K7 RESEARCH INTERESTS: Medieval and Renaissance confraternities and other such organizations of lay piety ACTIVITIES: occasional conferences; publication of *Confraternitas*; communication network among scholars working on confraternities in different disciplines (history, literature, religious thought, fine arts, music, etc.) COURSES: nil FELLOWSHIPS: nil

Index

The numbers in this index refer to entry numbers, not to page numbers.

Anglo-Saxon
  Archeology 48
  Literature 48
Archaeology 48, 199
Architecture 31, 43
  Italian 66
  Theatre 55
Archives
  Rome 178
Ariosto 159
Aristotle
  texts and commentaries 159
Art 28, 31, 32, 46, 72, 80, 120, 121, 127, 132, 144, 158, 172, 178, 194
  Italian 16, 96
  Lombard 133
  Post-Byzantine 129
Australia
  Sydney 14
Austria
  Krems an der Donau 111

Bacon, Francis 97, 98
Bandello, Matteo 61
Baronio, card. Cesare 56
Baroque 31
Baroque arts 31
Belgium
  Antwerp 75
  Bruxelles 114, 138
  Liège 91, 104
  Louvain 108, 181
  Louvain-la-Neuve 102

Tournai 195
Beverland 114
Beza 103
Boccaccio 3
Books 29, 100
Borthwick 17
Bucer 18, 49, 103
Buonarroti family 87
Burckhardt 1, 119

Calvin 49, 103, 150
Canada
    Calgary 139
    Kingston 20
    Montreal 105
    Ottawa 15, 19, 155, 168
    Sherbrooke 41
    Toronto 46, 49, 121, 162, 166, 175, 208, 214
    Vancouver 79
    Winnipeg 143
Censorship 41
Champagne 39
Cistercian art 48
City, medieval 48
Civilization 101, 120, 179
Commedia dell'Arte 55
Confraternities 214
Conservation 80
Contact, Europe-New World 29
Controversies, religious 103
Counter-Reformation 40, 56, 116
Courses 5, 6, 17, 21, 23, 24, 29, 31, 34, 36, 41, 42, 43, 46, 47, 48, 49, 51, 52,
    56, 59, 66, 79, 80, 86, 93, 94, 101, 102, 103, 104, 105, 108, 109, 113, 115,
    116, 119, 126, 131, 132, 133, 135, 141, 143, 144, 145, 147, 148, 162, 164,
    165, 170, 175, 178, 179, 181, 184, 185, 189, 197, 210, 211
Courts 72, 121
Culture 193
    English 97
    Medieval 147
    Portuguese 117
Cusa, Nicholas of 4, 81

Dance 30

De Ste Aldegonde, Marnix 114
Denmark
   Copenhagen 82, 96, 179
Diaspora, Greek 129
Dissent
   religious 103
Drama 47, 140, 142, 168
   Dutch 75
   Elizabethan 83
   English 159, 166
   Shakespearean 183
   Spanish 159

East-West relations 39
Education 29, 104
Elzevier 159
England
   Birmingham 185
   Egham (Surrey) 161, 201
   Hindhead, Surrey 84
   Leeds 47, 202
   Leicester 140
   London 80, 98, 99, 115, 198, 199, 210
   Oxford 85, 157
   Stratford-upon-Avon 123, 184, 185
   York 17, 48
Epistolography
   Humanist 114
Erasmus 5, 34, 49, 88, 89, 104, 114
Exegesis, biblical 103

Feasts 55
Fellowships 5, 9, 17, 22, 23, 27, 29, 31, 33, 34, 43, 46, 48, 49, 55, 57, 75, 86,
      93, 102, 103, 110, 115, 116, 119, 128, 129, 131, 132, 136, 144, 145, 147,
      150, 165, 176, 178, 179, 181, 184, 185, 187, 197, 203, 209, 210, 211
France
   Angers 5
   Grenoble 34
   Lyon 11
   Montpellier 42, 44
   Paris 13, 35, 36, 37, 40, 51, 52, 100, 167, 190, 191, 194, 196, 197
   Perpignan 125
   Rheims 39

Saint Mour 192
Saint-Etienne 101
Strasbourg 45
Tours 43
France, culture and civilization 11

Galileo 128
Galleries 80
Geography 99
Germany
    Bamberg 7
    Bergisch Gladbach 207
    Berlin 6
    Bochum 83
    Heidelberg 81
    Köln 160
    Mainz 110
    Marburg an der Lahn 182
    Münster 18
    Tübingen 113
    Wolfenbüttler 213
Greece
    Athens 38, 137

Hagiography 34
Henry VIII 5
Herbals 159
History 32, 46, 59, 82, 97, 121, 127, 132, 144, 147, 158, 172, 178, 187, 194
    Church 105, 110, 113, 144
    Cultural 63, 72, 210
    French 105
    German 136
    Institutional 72
    Intellectual 41, 145, 210
    Italian 136
    Oxford 157
    Portuguese 117
    Religious 17, 43, 104, 145
    Social 17, 72, 111
    Venetian 94
    War and Peace 36
Humanism 33, 49, 56, 67, 70, 100, 101, 116, 207
    Christian 104

Netherlands 114, 138
Humanities 28
Hungary
    Budapest 33

Instruments 84
Italy
    Bergamo 62
    Bologna 8, 90
    Ferrara 92, 127
    Firenze 55, 73, 87, 124, 130, 131, 209
    Fisciano (SA) 59
    Messina 63
    Milano 53, 71, 133
    Moncallieri (Torino) 64
    Napoli 132
    Padova 69, 70
    Perugia 54, 68
    Pisa 128
    Roma 1, 16, 58, 65, 67, 74, 95, 119, 126, 134, 135, 178, 189
    San Miniato (PI) 57
    Sora (Frosinone) 56
    Torino 188
    Tortona 61
    Trento 72, 136
    Urbino 2
    Venezia 94, 129
    Vicenza 66

Japan
    Tokyo 170
    travel to 160
    Yokohama 193
Journal
    Annali del centro di studi soriani 56
    Annali dell'Istituto Storico ... 136
    Annual Bulletin of the Milton Society 152
    Archivio di Filosofia 67
    Arte lombarda 133
    Baconiana 98
    Beihefte 110
    Bibliographie internat. de l'Humanisme ... 100
    Bibliothèque d'Humanisme et Renaissance 12

Bollettino dell'Istit. Storico Ital. ... 135
Borthwick Institute Bulletin 17
Bulletin de la Soc. de l'Histoire ... 191
Bulletin of the Shakespeare Association 183
Bulletin Réforme, Humanisme, Renaissance 11
Cahiers Elisabéthains 42
Cahiers V.L. Saulnier 52
Calvin Theological Journal 150
Comitatus 22
Deutsche Shakespeare-Gesellschaft Jahrbuch 83
Emblematica 144
Encomia 121
Epetiris 137
Erasmus of Rotterdam Society Yearbook 89
Etudes Champenoises 39
European Medieval Theatre 125
Explorations ... 203
Gesta 120
Historical Research 115
Humanistica Lovaniensia 181
I Tatti Studies 209
Il Flauto Dolce 189
Jottings 98
Journal of Medieval and Renaissance Studies 23
Journal of Renaissance Studies 201
Journal of the Lute Society of America 139
Journal of the Soc. for Post Medieval Archeology 199
Journal of the Southwest 177
Journal of the Warburg and Courtauld Institutes 80, 210
La Voce 119
Latomus 195
Machiavelli Studies 122
Mediaeval Studies 46
Mediaevalia 21
Mediaevalia Lovaniensia 108
Medieval Archaeology 198
Medieval Prosopography 147
Medieval Studies 162
Medioevo 70
Medium AEvum 202
Messaionika kai nea Hellenika 38
Misure critiche 59
Mitteilungen 182

Moreana 5
Newsletter 150
Nouvelle Revue du Seizième Siècle 12
Nouvelle Revue du XVIe Siècle 196
Parergon 14
Physis 128
Prospectus 80
Quaderni 132
Quellen ... 134
REED Newsletter 166
Renaissance and Reformation / Renaissance et Reforme 20, 49, 155, 208
Renaissance Drama 29
Renaissance News 170
Renaissance Quarterly 173
Renæssancestudier 96
Répertoire international des Seiziémistes 101
Research Opportunities ... 142
Revista de Historia das Ideias 116
Revue d'Histoire des Textes 100
Revue des amis de Ronsard 193
Revue Romane 179
Rinascimento 131
Rivista di Filologia Umanistica 63
Römisches Jahrbuch für Kunstgeschichte 16
Schifanoia 127
Scintilla 46
Shakespeare Quarterly 93
Sixteenth Century Journal 187
Studi Tassiani 62
Studies in Medieval and Renaissance History 79
The Consort 84
The Renaissance Bulletin 170
Thesaurismata 129
Thomas-Morus-Jahrbuch 207
Veröffentlichungen ... 111
Veröffentlichungen 110
Viator 22
Voce delle Arti e delle Lettere 1
Vortrage 110
Wolfenbüttler Renaissance Mitteilungen 213
XVIIe Siècle 194

Latin, Medieval 46

Law 28
Leonardo 10
Levant 129
Lipsius, Justus 114, 138
Literature 29, 39, 46, 50, 59, 63, 100, 121, 127, 132, 172, 178, 179, 193, 194,
    202
  Elizabethan 97
  English 158
  English Recusant 170
  French 43, 105
  Italian 6, 96, 160
  Jacobean 97
  Narrative 101
  Neo-latin 96, 138, 159, 181
  Polemical 52, 101
  Portuguese 117
Locke, John 103
Luther 104

Machiavelli 122
Manuals, school 104
Manuscripts 100
Marino 6
Max Planck Institut 16
Medicine 45
Milton 152
Monasticism
  English 48
Montaigne 192
More, Thomas 5, 207
Music 30, 32, 73, 84, 86, 126, 139, 161, 189
Music records 86
Musicology 43, 46, 127

Neo-Latin 181, 190, 195
Neo-platonism
  Florentine 160
Netherlands
  Amsterdam 88
  Leiden 211
Newsletter 5, 20, 29, 46, 49, 66, 78, 169, 199, 205
  Bollettino 56, 61
  Bulletin 201

Bulletin Burckhardt 119
Burckhardt 1
Canadian Rhetoric Newsletter 19
Confraternitas 214
CRR Newsletter 27
EDAM 147
Historians of Early Modern Europe 187
IMCS Newsletter 120
IRIS 107
Notiziario di San Giorgio 94
Nouvelles 24
Nouvelles des empreints 100
Nouvelles du livre ancien 100
Old English Newsletter 21
Renaissance News and Notes 173
The Bulletin 84
Vox Mediaevalis 147
Novellistica 61

Painting
Dutch 31
Paleography 17, 27, 29, 46
Palestrina 95
Palladio 66
Patristics 105
Pedagogy 104
Petrarch 6, 160
Petrarchism 160
Philology 59, 63
Philosophy 43, 46, 50, 53, 70, 71, 105, 117, 132, 147, 172, 194
Aristotelian 69
Plainsong 161
Poetry
Chivalric 6
Lyric 6
Poland
Warsaw 78
Political Science 71
Portugal
Coimbra 116
Lisbon 117
Printing
Greek 129

Proceedings 24, 93, 102, 118, 122
Prophétisme 36
Protestantism 44

Raphael 2
Reformation 27, 33, 40, 44, 78, 103, 110, 112, 113, 116, 147, 155, 200, 208
    English 48
    France 191
    German 49
    Protestant 27
    Swiss 49
Religion 71
Rhetoric 19, 50, 124
Richard III 176
Riche, Barnabe 15
Rome
    Renaissance and Baroque 58
Ronsard 193

Schools
    Latin 104
Science 9, 28, 50, 53, 97, 105, 128, 144, 172
Series 39
    Acta 21
    actes 39, 196, 197
    Actes des colloques 11
    Armonia Strumentale 189
    Astraea 42
    Bibliographie ... 114, 138
    Bibliographies 178
    Biblioteca del Cinquecento 72
    Bibliotheca Calviniana 150
    Bibliotheca dissentium 103
    Bibliotheca Hungarica Antiqua 33
    Bibliotheca Scriptorum Medii Recentisque Aevorum 33
    Bibliotheca Unitariorum 33
    Borthwick Papers 17
    Borthwick Texts and Calendars 17
    Borthwick Wallets 17
    Cahiers de la Renaissance Italienne 40
    Carleton Renaissance Plays in Translation 168
    Carteggi Umanistici 131
    Carteggio di Michelangelo 131

catalogues 97
Catalogus Translationum 103
Classica et Mediaevalia 82
Classici del Pensiero Italiano 67
Collana di Studi e Testi 2
Collection du Centre d'Etudes de la Renaissance 41
Collection Latomus 195
collections of essays 9
Corpus Catholicorum 103
Corpus inscriptionum 109
Corpus Palladianum 66
Corpus Platonicum Medii Aevi 210
Corpus Reformatorum Italicorum 29
Correspondance d'Erasme 114
Diálogos ... 116
Directory/Repertoire 20
documents 157
Early Drama Art and Music 147
Early Music Studies 86
Erasmi Opera Omnia 103
Estienne Gilson Series 162
exhibition catalogues 87
facsimiles 95
Fonti e Studi Baroniani 56
Fonti per la Storia d'Italia 135
guidebooks 184
Guides to research 27
Hakluyt Society Publications 99
Humanizmus es Reformacio 33
Index des livres interdits 41
Instrumenta humanistica 114
Iusti Lipsi Epistolae 114
Leeds Medieval Studies 47
Malone Society Reprints 140
MARC monographs 141
Martin Bucers Deutsche Schriften 18
Martini Buceri Opera Latina 103
Medieval and Renaissance Studies 210
Medieval and Renaissance Studies monographs 23
Medieval and Renaissance Texts and Studies 21
Memoria Saeculorum Hungariae 33
Monographs 5, 23, 127, 129, 198, 202, 211
Music: Scholarship and Performance 86

Musiche da suonare 189
Nordic Literature in Latin 96
Occasional Publications 49
Old English Dictionary 46
Opera Erasmi Roterodami 88
Opus Epistolarum Iusti Lipsi 138
Oxford-Warburg Studies 210
Pegasus Paperbooks 21
Portugiesische Forschungen ... 117
proceedings 24, 48, 57, 58, 61, 74, 77, 89, 93, 94, 95, 123, 131, 178, 189, 211, 212
Publications in Mediaeval Studies 145
Quaderni 136
Quaderni del Rinascimento 131
Records of Early English Drama 46, 166
Regesta Chartarum Italiae 135
Régi Magyar Költok Tara 33
Renaissance and Reformation Texts in Translation 49
Renaissance Monographs 170
Repertorium Fontium Historiae Medii Aevi 135
Report of the International Shakespeare Conference 185
Rerum Italicarum Scriptores 135
RIDS 179
Romansk Bibliotek 179
Runessansu Sousho 170
Sixteenth Century Bibliography 27
Sixteenth Century Essays and Studies 187
Spicilegium Friburgense 109
Studi e testi 63, 131
Studi storici 135
Studia Humanitatis 33
Studies in Medieval Culture 147
Studies of the Warburg Institute 210
Studio fiorentino 131
Subsidia Mediaevalia 162
Supplementa ... 181
Testi umanistici sulla retorica 67
textes 34, 43, 50, 102, 105
textes et études 51
texts 61, 73, 75, 85, 90, 127, 136, 145
texts and editions 132
texts and studies 178
Toronto Medieval Bibliographies 46

Toronto Medieval Latin Texts 46, 162
Toronto Medieval Texts and Translations 46
Toronto Old English Series 46
travaux 38, 101, 104, 105, 114
Typologie des sources du Moyen Age Occidental 102
Umanisti di Ciociaria 56
Warburg Institute Surveys and Texts 21
Shakespeare 9, 42, 83, 93, 98, 123, 159, 170, 183-185, 212
Slavic studies 46
Spain 35
Spenser, Edmund 206
Spirituality 104
STC books 159
Switzerland
    Fribourg 109
    Geneva 12, 103
    Zürich 50, 112

Tasso 159
    Bernardo 62
    Torquato 62
Technology 9
Theatre 47, 74, 101, 125, 130, 184, 185
    Commedia dell'Arte 55
    Dutch 75
    English 43
    Religious 34
Theology 29, 46, 104, 117, 147
Translations
    Humanist 96
    Church Fathers 103
Travel 64, 99, 106, 160
Turrettini, Jean-Alphonse 103

Urban studies 132, 178
Urbino 2
USA
    Albany (NY) 107
    Ann Arbor (MI) 141
    Binghamton (NY) 21
    Bloomington, (IN) 86
    Boston (Mass) 180
    Bronx (NY) 26

Chicago (IL) 29, 171, 172
Claremont (CA) 97, 169
College Park (MD) 28
College Station (TX) 203
Columbia (MO) 32, 206
Columbus (OH) 24
Dallas (TX) 146
Davis (CA) 156
Durham (NC) 23
Fort Washington (MD) 89
Gainesville (FL) 106
Greenvale (NY) 4
Honolulu (HW) 214
Kalamazoo (MI) 147
Kirksville (MO) 187
Los Angeles (CA) 10, 22
Minneapolis (MN) 30
Morgantown (WV) 212
Nashville (TN) 183
New Haven (CT) 165, 174
New Orleans (LA) 122
New York (NY) 76, 120, 142, 154, 173
Notre Dame (IN) 145
Philadelphia (PA) 151, 159
Pittsburgh (PA) 25, 144, 152
Plymouth (NH) 148
Portland (OR) 158
Princeton (NJ) 163, 186
Rochester, NY 118
Sarasota (FL) 164
St Louis (MO) 3, 27, 200
Tempe (AZ) 9
Tucson (AZ) 177
University (AL) 204
University Park (PA) 31
Upper Montclair (NJ) 176
Washington (DC) 93
Whittier (CA) 205
Williamstown (Mass) 153
USSR
Moscow 77

Vatican City 149

Vieira, F. Antonio 117

Waldesians 188
Women 180
   Danish 96

Zwingli 49

DATE DUE

MY 28 96			